Dinah Maria Mulock Craik

Fair France. Impressions of a Traveler

Dinah Maria Mulock Craik

Fair France. Impressions of a Traveler

ISBN/EAN: 9783337241667

Printed in Europe, USA, Canada, Australia, Japan

Cover: Foto ©Andreas Hilbeck / pixelio.de

More available books at **www.hansebooks.com**

FAIR FRANCE.

IMPRESSIONS OF A TRAVELLER.

BY THE AUTHOR OF

"JOHN HALIFAX, GENTLEMAN,"

"A BRAVE LADY," "OLIVE," &c.

NEW YORK:
HARPER & BROTHERS, PUBLISHERS,
FRANKLIN SQUARE.
1871.

I inscribe "Fair France"—France of yesterday—to those heroic and suffering souls in the France of to-day, who yet suffer in hope, seeing light through the darkness, and believing in a new and nobler France of to-morrow.

THE AUTHOR.

CONTENTS.

CHAPTER	PAGE
I. AT PARIS	9
II. IN THE PROVINCES	39
III. A CITY AT PLAY	76
IV. A PARIS SUNDAY	96
V. AN OLD FRENCH TOWN	119
VI. WE FOUR IN NORMANDY.—PARIS.—CAEN.—BAYEUX.—ST. LO.	146
VII. ST. LO.—COUTANCES.—GRANVILLE.—AVRANCHES	165
VIII. MONT ST. MICHEL	186
IX. AVRANCHES.—PONTORSON.—DOL.—ST. MALO.—DINAN	216

FAIR FRANCE.

CHAPTER I.

AT PARIS.

Until this year (1867) I used to boast, with pardonable or unpardonable conceit, of being one of the very few Britons who have never quitted their native shores. In short, I had never been, nor cared to go, abroad. A condition much reviled and reasoned against by affectionate friends, foreign and English; the former throwing out gentle hints about "narrow-mindedness," "insular prejudices," and so on; the latter enlarging on the endless delights of Continental traveling: in the course of which, however, both sides betrayed unconsciously so much that was any thing but delightful, that the skeptic became more skeptical than ever. At length Fate, acting by the tender compulsion with which she does act sometimes, driving us almost against our will to our best interest and keenest enjoyment, smoothed the way toward conversion; and one April day the infidel found herself—scarcely by her own volition, but still without unnecessary repining—on board of a Calais packet.

I make this preface as a sort of apology for writing on what all the world has already written upon, and chronicling sights which every body has seen. But not every body sees things with his or her individual eyes instead of another's; and to go out of one's own country for the first time, with vision fresh as a child's, yet with the experienced observation natural and necessary to middle life, is a combination rather rare. Therefore let me, too, have my little say, in the hope that there may be in it some few things worth saying, even upon such a threadbare topic as Continental traveling.

To begin at the beginning. People who have been abroad so early and so often that the original sensation is quite lost, can not realize what it is first to set foot on a foreign country, not as an enthusiastic, impressible young person, but a grown-up Briton, with one's British prejudices thick and strong—arming one's self against all possible and impossible evils, until one begins to feel like Don Quixote with his windmill, that it is running a tilt against perfectly imaginary foes. I shall never forget the sense of mingled amusement and humiliation which came over me when, on airing my innocent French in its native clime by some simple sentence concerning luggage, I was answered, "Madame will find it in de next room." And when the first fellow-passenger that sat down by Madame—who had not yet opened her lips—inquired, in the politest of broken English, "whether she had ever been in France before?" Madame altogether resigned herself to her destiny. Her French fellow-creatures appeared to her much like any others; but she felt convinced that she herself must to them bear the mark of the beast—bovine, though it only seemed to secure to her—would that John Bull would profit by the lesson when he receives foreigners at home!—an extra share of lenient courtesy and kindly consideration.

So here we are at last in *la belle France!* Strange misnomer! What ugly colorless levels of land does that driving rain sweep over! mixing earth and sky in one settled "smudge" of unpleasant neutral tint. The face of the country has absolutely no features at all—never could have, we doubt, under the most favorable weather. For hours we see nothing except forlorn fields, crossed now and then by long double rows of trees, stuck in like pegs in a cribbage-board, and here and there a house or collection of houses, uglier than the very ugliest village in the most commonplace parts of England. If this is *la belle France!*—But let us not be hasty of judgment. The one secret of going abroad with any comfort or advantage is to start with a determination to see, not the worst, but the best of the land and its inhabitants. We do not go to visit a neighbor in order to pick holes in him and his establishment when we come home.

Nearing Amiens, we begin to perceive, without doubt, that we are in a foreign country. True, the landscape is not unlike our English rural landscape when especially inane, and the farm-houses and buildings are like most others we know; but there is dawning a difference. For instance, in England, we never saw those huge, queerly-harnessed horses, with great sheep-skins hung at their necks, on the top of their collars, and bits of shiny brass dangling and jangling about their fore legs in a fashion which British Dobbin would never submit to for an instant. And our indigenous Hodge—how very unlike him is this Norman peasant, in his invariable blue blouse, which dots the view with a bit of refreshing color! He just stops in his plowing or wagon-driving—and what queer-shaped wagons they are!—to look up as the train skims by; and if near enough, we perceive that he is spare-made, sharp-featured, generally bearded, but has a neatness of costume and intelligence of face rather beyond Hodge's. It sets us moralizing and speculating on his daily life—what sort of cottage or hovel he lives in; what kind of people are his wife and children; and whether, supposing we were to drop in upon them at their supper to-night, we should understand them, or they us, in language, habits, or sympathies, any more than if we had dropped from the moon. This, with only an hour and a half of sea running between the two countries! It takes down our insular pride considerably.

The rain lasted till we came within a few leagues from Paris. Then it ceased; and after safely extricating ourselves from the wild whirl of the *douane*, so trying to John Bull's temper, we passed through a dazzle of shops just kindling their gas in the clear evening twilight, and took refuge in the sober-gray comfortable shadows of the Rue St. Honoré.

I shall always like that street—grave, quaint, narrow, with the dignity of the *ancien régime* in its very name. I had French ancestors who doubtless walked there, and shopped there, buying brocades and fans, and high-heeled shoes, full-bottomed wigs, rapiers, and swords; nay, perhaps shed a few drops of honest Huguenot blood there in the sad Saint Bartholomew days, though the history of France was yet clear of guillotines and *coups d'état*, and its old men could not say, as I heard an old man say once, "Which revolution? I remember four."

Nothing could look more anti-revolutionary than this quiet old street, in which we are now sheltered from all the foreboded terrors of Paris in the Exposition time, for three peaceful days. Ay, peaceful, full of the glorious independence of total strangerdom, floating about wide brilliant Paris like two pieces of drift-wood caught in and amused by any passing current, yet quite free of, and indifferent to, every thing beyond the surface. No, not exactly. There are two ways of traveling: simply to see places, to carry away in one's head a grand muddle of towns, churches, picture-galleries; a dead weight of tourist experiences, as cumbrous and lifeless, I was going to say as useless as a museum of stuffed animals; or else to see human nature, that wondrous mystery and most difficult study, of which we never can come to the end. We preferred the latter course. Consequently, it did not much matter that our first plunge into Paris was at nine o'clock at night—a soft, warm, spring night—with the glittering shops of the Rue de Rivoli on one hand and the dim glow of the Tuileries Gardens on the other, while up and down, between light and shadow, flowed the continual human stream, at first so like, but, when analyzed, so unlike that which keeps rolling along our London thoroughfares from dawn till eve, almost from eve till dawn.

To mingle in this French crowd was, I own, an entirely new sensation. All was so bright, so pretty, so gay; it felt exactly like a scene in a play. We Englishwomen seldom walk after dark in the streets of our great cities, unless quite obliged, and then we hurry through them, for there is little to attract and much to repel.

The lazy gaslight-strolling, the gay out-of-door evening life that seems to go on in Paris, and among a very respectable class too, is to us unknown, nay, impossible. Only fancy a well-to-do Bond Street tradesman sitting with his family sipping their social tea, and taking a friend or two to join therein on the pavement of Regent Street quadrant, exposed to the gaze of all passers-by! And what decent English maid-servant would choose to saunter bonnetless, shawlless, on her sweetheart's arm, staring in at the Strand shop-windows? Yet here they were, men and women, *bonnes, ouvriers, boutiquiers,* every rank of the *bourgeois* class apparently, their day's work done, all strolling about, bent upon enjoying themselves. And nothing could be more innocently enjoyable than to watch them doing it. The women, in neat, spotless white caps, young and old, pretty or ugly (though I declare I never saw one really ugly woman all the time I was in Paris, for the very poorest and plainest of them were neat and clean); the men, acute of face, tidy of dress, and oh! so polite of manner; you overheard the very lowest of them addressing one another as "Monsieur" and "Madame," and bowing or exchanging the civil hand-shake, which seems even commoner in France than with us, for the British workman considers it superfluous to greet his comrade with any thing warmer than a nod of the head, and a gruff "How do, Bill?"

Perfect as we think ourselves, our lower orders might learn a good lesson from the Parisians. How much better, for instance, is a recognized costume, plain and neat, of the whole servant class, than the tawdry finery that our maid-servants indulge in! If they only knew how much more suitable—nay, to touch still deeper the feminine soul—how much more becoming is the snow-white cap—what splendid *blanchisseuses* these Paris women must be!—than the tawdry bonnet stuck over with sham lace, and dirty artificial flowers. And what possible harm can it do a man to greet his neighbor civilly, even ultra-politely, rather than grumpily? Why should he not, after work-hours are over, wear a cheery face instead of a sullen one, and enjoy himself as much as he can?

I own I like enjoyment; I admire the sunshiny spirit within which teaches us how to make the best of things without. And I appreciate keenly the small passing civilities—the decimal coinage of daily life, so easy to count and carry about; worth little in themselves, but very useful for the time being. I may not always have a chance of receiving or offering a louis d'or (pardon!—I forget they are now all napoleons), but I can at any time buy a cup of delicious *café* for half a franc, or make a beggar happy with a few centimes. As a wise French friend said one day to me, "The difference between you and us is, that you try to make life difficult; we prefer it easy. You go about critically, looking out for the bad points in every thing and every body you meet; we are content with their good ones. We *like* to be happy; you are never quite sure that you ought not to be miserable. You are very good people, you English; but could you not be good in a pleasanter way?"

Perhaps it was the faint stirring of the mercurial "frivolous" ancestral blood, but I own I was touched by the sprightly pleasantness of these Parisians. What their undercurrent of life may be—whether fair or foul

—heaven knows; but outside there is a cheeriness which contrasts strongly with the sulky sadness or worn-out sharpness of the faces one sees in London streets and London shops. The shops here — all windows — with half the available stock exhibited therein—the best on the outside, as seems the universal way in Paris—these shops alone were a pleasant sight, especially with madame the shop-mistress sitting behind — well-dressed, well-looking—her selling ended for the day; knitting or sewing, while she has what across the Tweed we should call a "crack" with some neighbor as chatty, as polite, and as pleasant-looking as herself. In public, of course —every thing is done in public in Paris—and under the very glare of the gaslight; but madame is quite used to that. Privacy, of any sort or kind, is apparently neither expected nor desired in this curious country, which, with so narrow a line of sea between, seems in many things the very antipodes of our own.

This fact began to strike me more and more when, next morning, we went into that solemn old church of St. Roch, in the Rue St. Honoré.

It so happened—without any bigoted intentional avoidance—that never in my life had I been inside a Roman Catholic church. The Presbyterian spirit (not creed, to which I do not own) is perhaps the most opposite conceivable to the spirit of that religion which we Protestants, ignoring the obligations of centuries, are prone to call, insultingly, "Popery," and abhor and abuse with a virulence proverbial to those animosities which arise between kindred, or between foes who have once been friends. And yet, for me, I must confess that, having now seen a good deal of Roman Catholicism as it exists in France—the established worship of the people—I have come away with much more respect for it, much more tolerance—even some sympathy—and yet with a greater objection to it than ever, and a more earnest wish that it may never advance one step more in our own land. I can hardly account for this anomaly of feeling, except by the same peculiarity that would force one to be doubly just to one's enemies, and doubly careful in judging a person toward whom one was conscious of feeling a vague dislike.

Nothing can be more opposed to our English devotional idea than this French church—wide, vaulted, full of gilding and ornament; adorned with painting and sculpture like a heathen temple; sprinkled over with chairs like a concert-room, and circled with an outer stream of people perpetually walking about and staring around them—at the chapels, the pictures, the service, and the worshipers. These latter, all kneeling, and absorbed, every one of them, in an intensity of devotion that there is no mistaking, and which can not possibly be pretense, affect us most of all. I do not care, comparatively, for the fine architecture, the beautiful painted glass, with its "dim, religious light," the extraordinarily decked little chapels, and the high altar, with its huge red cross upon a black ground—all these are sensuous externalities; but I do care extremely for the spiritual and human element we find here—the atmosphere of earnestness and prayer which seemed to pervade the place. "Prayer — to images!" the anti-Popery reader will indignantly exclaim. Well, perhaps so. But in many of our churches nobody attempts to pray at all. In Scotland they stand still, and are prayed to. In England they sit still, and are prayed for. Now these people, old and young, rich and poor, come into the churches, and kneel down and pray for themselves. True, it is with fingers pattering over beads, and eyes lifted up to silly little Blessed Virgins of white plaster, belaced and becrowned; but oh! the eagerness of the faces! Some, hid in retired corners, seemed to carry with them such a weight of grief, of entreaty, of faith, and lay it down at the feet of those helpless figures—those blank-smiling Marys, or most repulsive similitudes of our Lord—that one felt the Divine Spirit beyond it all must have pitied a worship so ignorant and yet so sincere.

Being Passion Week, the devotees were chiefly dressed in mourning; some very richly in silks and velvets; some in black gowns, evidently improvised for the occasion out of shabby wardrobes; and some of the very poorest made no attempt at it at all. They came just as they were—in their daily rags; though a Frenchwoman's inborn cleverness and sense of *comme il faut* seems to make her wear even her rags respectably, at least when she appears abroad.

I saw here none of the squalidness which one finds mixed up with the same depths of poverty in England. The lowest market-woman, coming in with her basket, setting it down on the church floor, and popping on her knees beside it—for the advantage of a *prie-dieu* costs a few sous—even she had always a clean cap on, and her dress, however common, was seldom either dirty or ragged. Besides these poor women, too, we noticed a good many children, also of the lowest class, but all very tidy —nay, some of them quite picturesque in their little scarlet *capuchons;* for of course they were chiefly girls; the male element—man or boy—being almost entirely absent from Roman Catholic congregations. They would come quietly in, stare about them a little, as children will, then kneel down and say their prayers with a decorous gravity, as if they really meant it and liked doing it.

And one can well imagine the effect made upon children's minds—and on those of the common people, who are so like children in many ways—by these large, dim, peaceful churches, filled with all sorts of pretty and awe-inspiring things, dainty Holy Families, large white Christs, sweet-smiling or sorrowful-looking saints, every nook of every chapel turned into a perfect nest of finery—tinsel, gilding, lace, and flowers. Probably the one only sight of the beautiful—or what seems to them such—which the lowest class in France ever get, is in their churches. But our corresponding class never get it at all.

Whatever we thought of the worship itself—the morning mass that was going on in two or three places in the church at once—of the intense devotion of the worshipers there could be no doubt. As for the various performances, to us they appeared meaningless, nay, ludicrous: mutterings in an unknown tongue—bowings and scrapings—triple tapping of breasts and elevating of hands and arms—sudden poppings down on one knee and poppings up again—only I do not like to ridicule, lest I should be wounding the feelings of some good Christian Catholic to whom they are sacred and dear. Still, to turn from these, and see the ecstasy of devotion on the faces of some of the worshipers, and the grave religiousness written on all, was a very remarkable thing. How they prayed—whether it was mere vain repetition, pattered over with a vague sense that they were thereby helping to " make their salvation," as they express it—we could not know; but undoubtedly these poor French people did really pray, looking, meanwhile, as if they believed they should be heard—which is more than can be said of many English and Protestant congregations.

I own they startled me. My preconceived idea of a Roman Catholic church was a mere show—the very essence of show and frippery. Plenty of this I found, it is true; but I also found something else, which I did not expect, and which made my heart swell, and inclined me to think more, not of the Roman Catholic Church, but of Him who is the Fountain of something diviner than all churches, who can use and mould all things—even bad things—so as to evolve good and neutralize evil. This feeling made me tread softly and reverently—as I think I would even in a Mohammedan mosque—rather than insult by word or look my brethren and fellow-creatures, who, however differently they worshiped, were worshiping one God, and doing it in earnest.

But we could not linger at St. Roch, for all Paris was before us, with only a day and a half into which to compress it. That we accomplished this; saw two or three other churches, including Notre Dame; taking "*courses*" between from the centre of old Paris to the Bois de Boulogne in the rapidly rising new city which the Emperor is making; even paid a flying visit to the Exposition, chiefly, I confess, in order to say we had been there, and to hug ourselves in insular conceit upon the vast superiority of our own—that all this was done, and thoroughly done, so far as it went, reflects, we feel, considerable credit upon our ingenuity. Still, it is impossible to give, or to retain, more than a mere impression of the day, in which every thing seems to me now like a "fleeting show" of wide, white streets, busy boulevards, green avenues, bright, hot, statue-decked squares, where one tried vainly to conjure up the rattle of the death-cart and the flash of the guillotine. Only for one moment—standing by Cleopatra's Needle, in the Place de la Concorde, where Marie Antoinette stood and looked with one flitting, farewell glance at those same green trees in the Tuileries Gardens—did the past appear at all possible or probable.

Yet these things have been—may be again, who knows? For under all the frivolity and easy *insouciance* of this strange French people lurks something of the tiger—the sudden spring, the mad thirst for blood. We could see it, we fancied, in not a few faces, chiefly of young *ouvriers* and artisans; keen, intelligent, discontented, fierce; men whose life is a struggle and repression; men whom one would not like to watch in a popular *émeute* or to meet at a barricade. We could comprehend how there is going on—as the French themselves own with bated breath—below that smooth surface of Parisian life, a perpetual seething and smouldering, not unlike Vesuvius underneath the vines of Portici. Whether the volcano will blaze out again, in our day or our children's, who can say?

We left the grand Exposition—that admirable sop to

Cerberus, which this year has occupied the attention of the whole French people, and flattered their national vanity by making them hosts to half the world—and took refuge in the cool gray shadows of the Louvre.

Every body knows the Louvre. I shall not particularize a single object there except one picture, which, to me, obliterated all the others—Murillo's celebrated "Assumption." Looking at it, one can comprehend the reason why Mariolatry has taken such a firm hold of the Roman Catholic mind—especially the female portion of it—because it touches upon the strongest instinct, the deepest passion, in a woman's breast. Mary Mother, in all her various phases, from the instant which Murillo has here so exquisitely caught, when her pure soul first begins to look forward ecstatically to its maternal hope, until the final moment when all hopes are gone, or changed into a faith diviner still—this mysterious life of motherhood, with its unutterable joy and never-ended suffering, which every woman somehow understands, comes as a sort of shield between poor human nature and the blaze of Deity. It may be a most heretical confession, but I can quite understand why sorrowful, weak, oppressed women, too ignorant to know God, too cowardly to dare to appeal to Him face to face, take to worshiping the Virgin Mary.

We floated down all the other pictures, many of them familiar from engravings, on a dim, sleepy wave of pleasant weariness, individualizing nothing. In fact, I am afraid I carried away little beyond the general impression of them, and the delicious quiet of the place. There were few visitors, too few to interfere with the numerous students busy at work in every *salon*. Lady-students predominated. We noticed, with amusement, that always in front of the most ambitious picture, and copying it upon the biggest canvas, was perched some female artist—often a funny little Frenchwoman, middle-aged and pathetically plain, yet with a toilette always careful—let us say *soignée*, which expresses it better—in spite of paint-stains and chalk-marks. Moreover, the work was very good, much better than that of the generality of lady-artists. It was impossible not to sympathize with these, who evidently earned their bread so hardly; toiling here all day, and going home at night to some humble chamber *au sixième;* living like solitary winter birds on a bare tree-top, in some out-of-the-world *quartier*, till perhaps, like the birds, they one day drop off it and vanish under the snows.

Of men copyists we saw but few, and these very second-rate. The cleverest had lost his right arm, and was painting industriously with his left. We were so interested in this, and by the intent expression of his gray, worn face, a little severe and saturnine—likewise perhaps by his rather shabby clothes—that we hazarded a brief remark, a question about some picture opposite. Probably he thought it interfered with his work, for he answered it so abruptly that we never ventured a second. I only name this as being the sole instance of *brusquerie*—it did not amount to incivility—that I ever met with from a Frenchman.

The day was declining, and we had seen more of French buildings than French people. We looked forward hopefully to the *table d'hôte;* but, alas! it proved to be almost exclusively English. The British tongue, with Yankee variations, echoed from every side of the *salle à manger;* nay, the very dishes, the half-raw "*bifsteck*," and the still more dreadful *gigot*, had a fatal presumption of being English, which we could not sufficiently deplore. One only *plat*—decidedly novel—a most extraordinary compound of cheese and cauliflowers, caught our insular palate, and has remained there in memory and hopeless admiration ever since.

There was nothing particularly to be admired in the company; indeed, I have now forgotten them all except two people—the only French people, I fancy, among the number.

They were, seemingly, a newly-married couple. He must have been somewhere about five-and-thirty, with a fine, clear-cut, clever face, or rather less merely "clever" than intellectual—of the *savant* kind, I should say. He had also a look of simplicity and goodness, and a certain largeness and nobility of outline—Norman French, after the type of the man in Millais's picture of the Huguenots. Indeed, there was an air of gentle blood about him, down to his very hands, which were handsomer than one usually sees in Frenchmen. For her—she was lovely; small, delicate, large-eyed; scarcely out of her teens, and as timid-looking as a young hare of the wood. She might never have been across her convent-gate, or out of her mother's sight till now, and she seemed to creep to her husband for protection against this terrible, unknown, outside world—though she was a little frightened of him, too; stole at him glances of shy strangeness, and colored sensitively almost every time he addressed her.

Obviously, one of those marriages, essentially French, which we English regard with such holy horror theoretically; though, practically, many of ours are not a whit better—a *mariage de convenance*, arranged by parents and friends, in which the bride has no voice whatever, nor dreams of having one. The pair were exceedingly courteous to one another, but had by no means that air of complete content—even silly content—which our English honeymoon couples show, perhaps a little too plainly. Yet there was something very touching in the quiet, protecting gravity of the bridegroom, the shy, sweet look of the bride. She did not dislike him, evidently—this gentle, honest-looking man, with twice her years, and probably thrice her cleverness; whom, in all probability, she had scarcely seen more than a few formal times before she was married to him. Poor little girl! I wondered what sort of woman she would grow up to, whether presently her shrinking shyness would all drop off, and she would blossom out into the married woman—the married Frenchwoman—according to our English ideal of the species (which, however, may be different from the reality)—lively, brilliant, entirely self-possessed; charming, and conscious of her charms; clever, and making the utmost use of her cleverness, and especially of those qualities in which she surpasses all civilized women—tact, *savoir faire*, and perfect knowledge of the world.

A character—you may like it or not; there is much to be said for and against it—which we quiet Englishwomen are prone to believe the natural outcome of that state of society in which *mariages de convenance* are the rule, and not, as we hope with us, the melancholy exception. The French argue that their system has its advantages. "Oh, I am sure to be married; we have no old maids in France," said to me a lively damsel of fifteen. Plain or pretty, all take their turn, and fulfill what is regarded as the natural destiny of women, without any of the bitter jealousies and souring disappointments which deteriorate the weaker sort of what are satirically called our "surplus females." Also, these plain, outspoken, matrimonial bargains, arranged by parents or friends, avoid at least the personal struggle after husbands which makes our young women often the mock of the other sex, and the humiliation of their own.

Heaven forbid I should be supposed to defend these "arranged" marriages; but, before we blame our neighbors, we should take care that our own hands are clean. I have seen in England many a sham sentimental, but in reality most mercenary union, where the woman seemed to have, and deserved to have, far less chance of happiness than this gentle little French bride. And, however unwise and dangerous may be the system of seclusion practiced toward young girls in France, taking them direct from the school-room to the altar, still, when I think of this young creature, and of other *demoiselles* I know, and compare them with certain "fast" young English ladies whom I have sometimes met, I confess it feels like turning from a bed of wild garlic in full flower—country readers will appreciate the force of the simile—to a bank of lilies of the valley, or a nooky hollow of blue and white violets.

After the *table d'hôte* we again threw ourselves into

the many-colored stream of Paris life, and were drifted on and on through the lighted streets, until we found ourselves a portion of the queer multitude which nightly sits sipping its *café noir*, or *café au lait*, in the square of the Palais Royal. Very curious it was to watch the various groups, and listen to their clatter of tongues. They were, apparently, of the shop-keeping class—decent, well-to-do families, who, in England, would retire to the little parlor behind, or take, after business hours, a quiet stroll in the parks, always ending in either their own or a neighbor's fireside. Here, no such privacy is ever thought of. "Home" is only *chez nous*—in reality as in word; and what to us is an Englishman's castle, his defense against all the world, would to a Frenchman be a sort of Brixton Penitentiary. Still, it is their way; it harms us not, and why should we condemn it? Only we should not like to follow it.

Passing the great gates of St. Roch, now closed for the first time in the day, we determined to go there again next morning. And so began a series of church visitations, which we agreed was the most interesting part of our traveling. Whenever we saw a church-door open, we went into it; rested from fatigue in its cool shadows, and studied life—lay and clerical—from the numberless points of view it afforded us. I can not say that it was to us, in any sense, a "place of worship;" though I believe an honest Protestant might say many an honest, reverent, humble prayer in a Catholic church; but it had a certain religious atmosphere which was soothing and sweet.

This morning at St. Roch is especially fixed on my

memory. Being Thursday in Passion Week, there was something special going on—what, we were too little acquainted with the Roman Catholic ritual to discover. I suspect it was a sort of service which is called *Ténèbres;* at least that was our impression, from the extreme and almost gloomy solemnity of the intoning and chanting which formed the greater part of it. It was listened to with earnest devotion by a large congregation, filling an inclosed space in front of the high altar. Before that altar were a number of officiating priests, busy in some performance or other. Oh, what a blaze of colors, what vestments, what embroidery and laces! How fine a thing it must seem to be a priest in the eyes of those little white-stoled boys who go swinging their censers backward and forward, filling the church with a luxurious odor, which, to a sensitive organization, is an intoxication itself! Undoubtedly the burning of perfumes in religious worship must be a lesson learned from ancient heathendom, which made all the senses subservient to the soul.

In addition to this stationary congregation within, a large ambulatory one was perpetually circulating in the outer area, or praying in the little chapels. A crowd, most conglomerate in character, rich and poor "meeting together," as if they really believed that "the Lord was the Maker of them all." Here, for instance, was an old, a very old woman, yellow as parchment, her nose and chin meeting like a witch's, her shabby clothes hanging round her shrunken shape as if upon a scarecrow, and her skinny hands clutching the dirty, tattered breviary that was almost dropping to pieces, leaf by leaf; while beside her, so close that the velvet mantle rubbed against the ragged shawl, knelt an elderly lady, dressed in the extreme of fashion, praying out of a splendid gold-embossed prayer-book. Yet the expression of both faces was strangely similar; in its intense absorption, its entire singleness of devotion. Neither noticed the other, though, as I said, their attire actually touched—nor did they notice us, though we stood a long time watching them, and finally left them still kneeling there.

In several chapels I had remarked a queer sort of double compartment, with a footstool in each division, and a pigeon-hole grating between. To one of these a very decent-looking, comely young woman walked up and knelt down. I followed, being curious to see what it was, till a severe "*Madame, c'est défendu,*" compelled my retiring. Soon, threading the crowd, came a priest in plain black and white vestments, no colors; a little, stout, common-looking man, round-faced, with no particular expression; I have seen his like in many a pulpit in our own land, and listened to many a dull, harmless sermon from the same. He passed into the inner box to where the young woman knelt, and then I knew I had been boldly marching into the very confessional.

The confession began. Of course, it was inaudible to me; but I could not keep my eyes from that kneeling figure—the face hidden, the shoulders actually shaking with excess of agitation. And when I thought of the stolid and stupid-looking man I had seen pass into the opposite pigeon-hole, I felt rising up a very un-Catholic spirit of disgust and indignation. What could this poor foolish priest, who was neither husband nor father, and had probably quite forgotten the relations of son or brother —what could he know of human nature, and, above all, of woman's nature, so as to comfort, absolve, or advise in any case of sin, or suffering, or wrong? The two most obnoxious points, to my mind, in the Roman Catholic Church—viz., the celibacy of the clergy, and the system of the confessional—came upon me with such force, that I should like to have gone up to the young woman and taken hold of her by those poor quivering shoulders, and said to her, "Don't be such a fool! Don't lean your faith upon any priest alive; carry your burden direct to Him who said to the weary-laden, 'Come.' Put no shield between you and God. A woman should confess her sins to no mortal man—except, perhaps, if he is worthy of it, her own husband. You poor visionary! rise up from your knees and go home."

Which excellent advice was, of course, neither given nor taken; and I had to move on in smothered indignation, for there was coming round a most magnificent personage, in such splendid attire that I first thought he must be some great officer of state, or Church dignitary —perhaps even the Archbishop of Paris himself—but he turned out to be nothing more than the *huissier* of St. Roch—that is, the beadle. This grand gentleman, wand in hand, preceded a mild-looking little old priest, who held out a bag for alms, and seldom in vain, even to the poorest. And when they had made the circuit of the church, they went back into its centre division, and the service commenced again.

The next half hour I shall not easily forget. The roll of the deep bass voices—such voices as I never heard before in cathedral, or opera, or oratorio—the mingled majesty and pathos of the music, also unlike any music I am acquainted with, as it came rising and falling, thrilling and sweeping through the arches of the dim, half-lit church—truly the inventors of masses, and Catholic ceremonials generally, knew well what they were about! Had I believed in all this, I should have been utterly overcome by it; and even as it was, not believing in it at all, convinced that it was just a beautiful meaningless show, it affected me to an almost painful degree. Nothing marvelous is there in the fits of ecstatic devotion under the influence of which young Catholics devote themselves for life to the service of the Church; become priests, and nuns, and Sisters of Charity. How easily might impressible minds mistake the raptures of mysticism for the calm, rational life which works itself out by the humble fulfillment of life's common duties! how naturally might they fancy they could please God and buy salvation by a passion of religious exaltation, or painful asceticism, rather than by the holy delights, and as holy self-denials, which He ordained for man's ordinary career on earth!

We were not near enough minutely to observe the officiating priests; but there seemed a great number of them, and an equal number of acolytes, or whatever they are called—boys and youths growing up to be priests. One could not help thinking what a heavy loss to France, as a country, all these vowed celibates must be: socially, even on the most matter-of-fact principles of political economy, how many useful masters, householders, and citizens are thus taken from the duties of the community. Morally, the loss is still worse. We Britons expect to find—and, to the credit of our clergy, we usually do find—in the minister of our parish a real man, with every good and manly quality fairly developed; a kindly neighbor; a tender husband; a father with a whole household of children to bring up, often through much poverty, in the way they should go; in many cases adding to these duties external and social ones, such as magistrate, landlord, and general referee. We feel our clergyman to be one of ourselves. We can talk to him and consult him; he can understand our difficulties and sympathize with our cares, for they are nearly the same as his own. But the French *curé*, be he ever so good and sincere a priest—as I believe many of them are—how can he possibly enter into these things? Men of God in all ages have often been solitary men — Elijahs and Pauls; but these are exceptional cases. The question is whether, viewed as a whole tribe—an integral portion of the community—the priesthood can serve God better as exceptional creatures leading exceptional lives, or as being one with their brethren—serving Him, the Father of all men, with their whole being, instead of only a part of it? Is it not through the sanctification of human nature, rather than the ignoring of it, that we attain to our nearest knowledge of things divine? From God to man, and from man back again to God, seems to be the law of the highest religious life; otherwise it degenerates into mere mysticism on the one hand, and mere morality on the other.

A long homily to spring from the text of this splendid ecclesiastical show! That it was a very beautiful show we could not deny; nor that there might be good in it, of some sort, to some people, since the mere act of faith is an ennobling thing, and almost any kind of worship is better than no worship at all. But when, coming out of the church, we met a child's coffin coming in—nobody's child in particular, I suppose, for it had a very humble following of mourners—I could not help thinking how petty was all this pomp of ceremonial compared with the little dead body lying under the white pall, or the little spirit far away who might now comprehend the secret of all things.

In an hour more we had quitted Paris, not very regretfully; for its white glaring streets began already to pall upon eyes most accustomed to green fields. It was infinitely refreshing to glide out—French railways never do any thing but glide—into the open country, where the Seine lay in broad, glittering, sunshiny sheets of water on either hand; and the pretty suburban villas and gardens, just like English gardens, with lilacs and laburnums in full bloom, began to grow sparser and sparser as we reached the open country—real country; the same familiar hedgerows; the same cowslips in the meadows and primroses on the banks; the same sudden blue of woods full of hyacinths as we passed; yet all this beauty was like Ophelia's rue—" worn with a difference."

I can not describe it—perhaps it was half imagination; but this day's sensations are never likely to come again until I get into Paradise. Every thing was so entirely new, with just enough of the old look of things remaining to remind one of the past. Yet the sense of novelty was not as it almost always is—to me, at least—

rather painful than otherwise. All the world looked so kindly, so lovely, that, though it was altogether strange, one lost that vague dread which always accompanies strangeness, and felt only as if one were born again, and began the world again, looking at it with all a child's fresh eyes. One wondered whether, in the unknown country, where we shall all some day wake up, perhaps as ignorant as little children, perhaps carrying with us some dim remembrance of a former state to guide us in the awful life to come wherein God "shall make all things new"—whether that marvelous awakening will be a sensation any thing like this?

But from such flights of fancy we were speedily dragged down by a clatter of conversation. Never, in any language, did I hear so many words crammed into a given space of time. The incessant *oui, oui, oui*, and *non, non, non, non*, where an Englishman would have contented himself with a single negative or affirmative—the shrugs, the gesticulations, the enormous amount of energy and vitality spent upon what seemed such a small necessity, were quite overpowering. I am sure those two Frenchmen, one of them in particular, talked more in three hours than an ordinary Briton would have done in three months—not uncleverly: the French have such a brilliant, graceful, and ingenious way of "putting things," even the smallest triviality. From our neighbors' voluminous and voluble gossip—more like a woman's gossip, though they were an elderly and a middle-aged gentleman—I could soon have learned, had I listened, which it was difficult to help doing, all the domestic and social history of the province.

Gradually, however, the talk veered round to politics. At the word Luxembourg, a silent old gentleman at our left hand, who had hitherto distinguished himself chiefly by taking out a huge pork pie and a huger clasp-knife, upon which he and a youth opposite lunched contentedly —this fat, round-faced, phlegmatic person turned round, his blue eyes glaring, and stammered out a question in the worst possible French. It was answered politely, of course; and the lively French gentleman took the utmost pains to make out his fellow-traveler's meaning. Others helped, and by degrees the whole carriage warmed up into sociability, and made frantic efforts at general conversation. This was difficult, seeing we were two French, two Germans, two English; the French could not speak a word of German or English, the Germans had no English and very little French, the English boasted about six words of German, and as to their French— well! the less conceited they were on that matter the better. Under these melancholy circumstances, the way in which we all six jabbered at one another—mutually interpreting or misinterpreting, and resorting mostly to the universal language of signs and smiles—luckily, a pleasant face needs no dictionary—was highly creditable to all parties; the more so, as every body being of strong and diametrically opposite politics, did not add to the calmness of conversation.

The Frenchman and the elderly German immediately split on the subject of Luxembourg. The former leaned forward, his black eyes darting fire, and his long mustache almost standing on end with excitement, and poured forth a torrent of words, happily half unintelligible. The latter sat back, glowing in a dumb white heat of wrath, and imitated the "click" of a musket as his only available expression of what every German meant to do to every Frenchman rather than resign Luxembourg; at which we all burst out laughing, or else, in plain English (which we found ourselves rapidly forgetting, and becoming polyglotized), the carriage would soon have been too hot to hold us.

Then general and domestic politics took the lead, and we all spoke our minds, and heard our opposite neighbors' minds pretty plainly. But as this is not the custom in France, and as much that was said was confided to English honor and English reticence, I will not repeat it, though it was the most interesting part of the journey. We turned from that smiling Normandy—its hills and its dales, its pastures and farms, its picturesque villages, towns, and churches, which we caught sight in passing, and hoped to see more of by-and-by—to the human elements around us; the strong national characteristics, which are the finest study of travelers. Of course, they were nothing to us, these strangers—met for an hour, and never to be met again—and yet we felt a vague kindly interest in the honest German, who had left his household behind him—and he evidently thought a good deal of *ma famille*—and was going to spend a week with his brother, settled here in France. Also with less sympathy, but a good deal of curiosity, we contemplated these first specimens of French gentlemen that we had come across — especially the younger one. He, as he talked, convinced us more than ever of what I have before named,—the tigerish element, which is never quite absent from the gay French nature. Looking at this man—smiling, courteous, kindly no doubt in his way, yet ready on occasion to blaze up into something which one would rather have in a friend than an enemy—we comprehended how *la Revolution* happened, and why it has changed into *une revolution*—no exceptional tempest, but a sort of every-day whirlwind, which comes to the French people as natural as the air they breathe. How long the next will be staved off—who knows?

The ice once broken, it was wonderful how friendly we all became, how patient of one another's obtrusive nationalities, though the Frenchmen did give a polite shrug or two, aside, at the German's extreme slowness, and the German, walking up and down a station, made two pathetic confidential complaints to us—of the impossibility of comprehending that fast-talking Frenchman, and of the extreme thinness of the Norman beer. Still, we amused ourselves much, and got out of one another an amount of cosmopolitan facts and feelings, enough to ponder and speculate on for many a day; and when we parted—never certainly to meet again in this world—it was with *adieux* and good wishes cordial as sincere; which, if any of them ever read this—almost an impossibility to suppose—we hereby beg to reindorse.

And so we came, full of cheery and kindly thoughts and pleasant expectations, to the first break in our journey, a station about half way on the Paris and Havre line. The country—and lovely country it is—lay spread out before us, with a sunshiny, welcoming smile; the clatter of strange tongues began to seem less unfamiliar; we had found out that French nature was human nature, just the same as our own. The great lesson for which one goes into a foreign country—to like it, to be content in it, to get over our prejudice against it, and grow humble, rather than proud, by comparisons, was beginning to be learned. *La belle France!* Yes, it was really so to us to-day. And to-morrow? But that must stand over for another chapter.

CHAPTER II.

IN THE PROVINCES.

Once more we are at the same junction station—small and quiet enough after London or Paris railways, though no doubt it forms a very important link of communication between the outside world and the inhabitants of this fair province of Normandy. I can imagine the perplexity of the quaint, sleepy, old-world town—existing much as it is now, apparently, since the Crusades—when the alarming *chemin de fer* first burst into it; and along those pleasant slopes, yellow with colza, or green with pasture-land, or reddening with growing hay, came snorting past the great bright beast, with white puffing breath and fiery eyes—the locomotive dragon which has been, not slain, but ridden and mastered by a new St. George. However, it has grown used to these marvels, the queer old town, which I do not intend to describe, nor even to name. Let it remain in the reticent sanctity under which we hide all most pleasant things.

Well, our visit to friends was over, and here we were once again—two British monads—adrift in this strange land. But it had grown familiar now. Since we landed at this place three weeks ago, there had come an interval, a hiatus—never to be put into print, but ever remembered — and therein we had gained much. We emerged from its deep peace to find ourselves foreigners, certainly—I doubt if ever the British nature could wholly amalgamate with another race—but strangers no more. Courageously speaking in French, we took our *billet* (the civil official again glancing at us, and putting in a perfectly unnecessary and humiliating "ye-es"), and ranged ourselves among the little crowd that waited for the Havre train—

A crowd as unlike that of an English terminus as possible. In the first place, our liberty (that rare commodity in France, concerning which a French innkeeper once said to me, "Madame, it is no matter; if we had it we should not know how to use it")—our liberty was completely taken from us. Likewise our luggage. Instead of following it, battling for it, snatching it from stray porters, and having no rest till it was safely deposited in the van, we get it weighed, pay a few *sous* for it, receive a small scrap of paper—on the production of which our right over it depends—and then, lo! it is taken clear out of our hands, and we might as well grieve after it as after last week. It has vanished completely, and in another minute we ourselves are caught and penned up, always politely, but very securely, in a double compartment, where first and second class are arranged separately, like superior and inferior animals, and have to remain so till an official throws the doors open, announcing "*le train.*"

I do not say this is a bad plan; for some things it is a better plan than ours; it avoids all the noise and confusion which make an English railway such a horror to nervous and fidgety folk; but still, we are English; we dislike having our freedom restricted; above all, we dislike having to come about half an hour before, and wait three quarters of an hour after the time for *le train*—which was late, of course; I think they always are in France. But nobody else seemed to mind this at all; the good Normans remained patient, with or without seats, and chatted together in the most *amiable* and *agréable* way. I use the words in their native signification, which is a shade different from ours, and peculiarly applicable to the French people, who seem to have the art of making life pass so much more smoothly than we do, of oiling its creaking wheels, and stepping lightly over its rough roads. Well, small blame to them; rather the contrary.

"*Messieurs les voyageurs*," as the French *affiches* gracefully translate our abrupt word "passengers," were of all sorts and classes. A good many artisans—one of these, with a pale young wife hanging after him, had that keen, dark, discontented look we had so often noticed among French *ouvriers:* I could well have conjured up over his thick black hair, fierce eyes, and long mustache, the terrible *bonnet rouge*. There were peasant-women in short petticoats, *sabots*, and the picturesque cap into which the high Norman head-dress has gradually dwindled. And there were several nuns, or, more likely, Sisters of Charity—common-looking, but fresh-faced and comfortable sort of women, fat and cheerful, and any thing but interesting, except in their costume.

Also, there was the other costume which meets one every where in France, that of the priest or *curé*—the shovel hat; the round black cape; and the womanish black petticoat, with its long tail tucked up behind. Most of these priests looked like what we universally heard they were in the provinces—men chiefly taken out of the peasant ranks, having a warm feeling for, and a wide influence among the class from which they spring, but very imperfectly educated, and of little originality or grasp of mind. Not at all the "ravening wolves" that our anti-papal parsons would make them out to be, but kindly, silly old sheep, whom only the warning bell round their necks could make distinguishable from the rest of the flock—very good fellows nevertheless, who would come and dine with you whenever you asked them, making no difference between Catholic or heretic; and, if you wanted it, would give you a dinner too, out of their humble store; for they are mostly as poor as Scotch ministers, and have as needy parishes, to which many of them devote themselves faithfully during their long, wifeless, childless lives. In one small village churchyard I remember stopping to look at the monument of the last *curé*, who, it is said, had been priest of the parish, universally beloved, for "*quarante-huit ans.*" Only fancy a man gifted with any brains, any human passions, leading such a life, in this remote corner, for nearly half a century! Truly, whatever the Reverend Boanerges Hate-the-Pope, or poor frightened Mrs. Anti-Ritual may say, I believe that, putting theology aside, there are worse people here and there in the world than these French *curés*.

They, the nuns, and the working-people were all together in a second-class pen; the first contained a sprinkling of the uncostumed "higher orders," who dress the same, and look pretty much the same all the world over. But in them we noticed little of the fine Norman face which had struck us so much in the common people. Scarcely in the women, who grow prematurely old and coarse, but in the men it was very remarkable—the clear blue eye, aquiline nose, and classical-shaped mouth. They were tall, too, and well made; indeed, both as to features and figure, many of the herdsmen and farm-laborers hereabout reminded us strongly of some of the old knights lying with their legs crossed in our English cathedrals; nay, the very coachman who drove us hither to-day might have stood, just as he was, about six feet three, fresh featured, high nosed, large handed, with the most gigantic *sabots* imaginable, for a model of our William the Conqueror.

That great hero, though we hardly recognized him as *Guillaume le Conquérant*, is a notable person in these parts, and we were bound to-day to his burial-place, Caen. It was with a queer feeling of being, somehow, back into the Middle Ages, with the past running continually in and out of the present, that we heard at last *le train*, and struggled in somehow, trusting our luggage to fate and a benign imperial government, and were whirled through this fair country, that lay brightening under the first really hot day of spring—quite English country, familiar and sweet, while in the time-table and at the small stations we found names belonging to the day of lesson-learning—Evreux, Falaise, Bayeux, and so on; places which hitherto had for us no existence save in Pinnock, and now we were really nearing them.

"Caen!"—unmistakably Caen. And with a vague doubt of the infallibility of government, I darted out and began the truly Anglican search after luggage, of which, like most foreign travelers, we now wished one half was at the bottom of the sea. In vain did more experienced wisdom insist that it was " only French ways," and would be sure to come right. I could not be comforted; the *bagages* were nowhere. At last a vociferous omnibus-man, finding out whither we were going, hauled us into his vehicle, snatched the crumpled scrap which was our only safeguard as to property, and vanished. How shall I describe the scene which followed!—the dreadful ten, twenty, nay, I believe it was thirty minutes — during which we sat broiling, in company with six Caennois— two of them very fat—who seemed to take it quite easily!—the mixture of wrath, despair, and total helplessness with which we regarded every thing French meanwhile —and the thrill of returning peace which came when we saw the man reappear, smiling—they always smile in France—with a sheaf of *billets* in his hand, and our luggage all safe! And now I aver, honestly, that I think, in this and some other disciplines, a benign imperial government is in the right of it. We know what *we* are— we English—at Euston, Paddington, or London Bridge; but only imagine a crowd of Frenchmen and Frenchwomen clamoring for their property. Babel would be let loose, and Chaos come again.

Caen is known to English people from there being here a Lycée where education for boys is both good and cheap, costing, I believe, not more than £30 a year. Consequently many poor gentlemen and gentlewomen with large families go there temporarily to reside, and make quite a little colony of Britons in this pleasant, healthful place. Caen has nothing very notable about it except its churches. These, especially the *Abbaye aux Hommes* and *Abbaye aux Dames*, built respectively by William the Conqueror and his queen in atonement for their having married within the prohibited degrees, we had been strictly charged to see. But at present our thoughts were engrossed in arriving safely at an inn. As we rolled down the narrow Rue St. Jean, under the archway which led to the court-yard of this one—where the entrance-hall, the *salle à manger*, the kitchen, and the stables seemed all to be side by side—we felt that we were now really in France. No more of those insultingly polite replies to our bad French in still worse English. "Put that down!" energetically said to two big Normans, who would insist on carrying a very small portmanteau between them, elicited only a broad stare. No, nobody understood English here. Our French must be risked. We must "do or die."

We did do, and we did not die. We shall always recall kindly that little Caen hôtel. Of course it had its defects. To British feet, a wide expanse of polished flooring, slippery as glass, on which one has to walk like a cat in pattens, is not agreeable at first. Also, one prefers washing out of something bigger than a cream-jug and a pudding-basin; and when, to the amazement of the *femme de chambre*, we order a fire—which consists of two logs of rather green wood laid across two bars of iron on the open hearth—the result does not quite satisfy a shivering Briton. Still, let us be cheerful—and French—for the nonce. So we make the best of every thing, and go down to our first *table d'hôte à la Française*.

The *salle à manger* is a large, square room, with glass

doors — not windows merely, but doors opening on to the street. It is furnished with a horse-shoe table and plenty of mirrors. Every where we noticed that, whatever else may be deficient in French hôtels, one is sure to find abundance of mirrors and ormolu clocks. At first the room is empty; but gradually come dropping in about a dozen Frenchmen. Not that they look very French: you might take them for stout Yorkshire squires or Manchester manufacturers. Few are bearded, none cigar-scented; indeed, here I beg to mention that in all my wanderings through France I was never once annoyed by smoking, which appeared much less general than in England. Presently more guests appear — ladies also, who hang up their bonnets on the pegs behind, and take their places unconcernedly at the table, as if it were their established custom. A few seem to know one another, and begin conversation; but mostly the table is very quiet, and every body's attention seems concentrated on the business of dinner.

A word here on these French dinners. I own, at first, they were to me a deep mystery. What could be the use of taking twelve different mouthfuls of twelve successive dishes? Why on earth could not one eat the meat and potatoes together, instead of gazing hungrily at a small fragment of *rôti* sitting forlorn in the middle of one's plate, to be followed, at long intervals, by a bite of fried potatoes and two tea-spoonsful of sorrel or spinach? It seemed such an awful waste of time and appetite. I will not deny, there have been moments when a good slice of roast beef and two honest potatoes, or even a substantial piece of bread and cheese and a glass of milk, and then to rise at once, one's dinner done, would have been a state of things quite paradisiacal. But shortly there grew to be a certain charm in these lengthy meals—these multifarious, varied, delicately-cooked dishes—in which one was always wondering what was to come next, and what it was made of when it did come. My domestic and culinary spirit began to have a secret admiration for the way in which French cooks contrive to make something out of nothing—to evolve the tastiest of dishes out of the most ordinary materials; also for a certain refinement of feeding, very pleasant in its way —no greasy nastiness of stews; no gigantic, ill-cooked joints; no swilling, during dinner and after, of heavy ale and porter, or well-brandied wines. Undoubtedly, as a nation, our neighbors are more temperate than we—in eating probably, most decidedly in drinking. While a Briton luxuriates in rich meat dinners, strong ales, and "heady" wines, a Frenchman lives upon dainty dishes, chiefly composed of vegetables, and drinks the lightest of *vin ordinaire*. Of course, either follows his own way of living, and thinks it the best way; still, on comparing the two, one feels inclined to believe that the chances of a healthy, enjoyable existence, blessed with a clear head and a sound stomach, are rather in favor of *Monsieur*.

To return to our Caen *table d'hôte*, where our landlord always gave us admirable dinners, and presided at them himself in a style of equal-handed justice quite inimitable. At the conclusion every body rose, resumed hats or bonnets, and silently disappeared. We too went out, in the soft April twilight, to make our first investigation of a real provincial French town. Well, "Murray" describes it; I need not. It was a queer enough feeling to be here in the heart of France, miles away from any familiar face or tongue, and to see all things going on around us, ripple after ripple succeeding one another on this light surface life, which we watched, amused as children almost, but of the inner depths of which we knew absolutely nothing.

First we came to what we supposed the market-square —a wide, open space, with a church in the centre. Outside the railing was a quaint little group—a blind fiddler, fiddling away between two lighted candles, which burnt steadily though dimly in the still air. On either side of him sat a man and woman, singing in concert some interminable ballad, quite composedly and contentedly, though nobody noticed them or gave them any thing. Outside, the architecture of the church looked magnificent in the warm sunset glow; inside, it was dark and desolate, except for three black figures kneeling before the high altar, and an old woman who came clattering up thither in her *sabots*. We went out again, and took our way through the cheerful evening streets, where the people stood chatting at their shop-doors, or began to stroll about in twos and threes.

We wished to find out the *Abbaye aux Hommes*, now the church of St. Etienne, where the Conqueror lies buried, and many a question we had to ask, to which we invariably got the fullest and civilest answers. And here I must candidly confess that one of the pleasantest things in *la belle France* is the exceeding politeness of what we call the "lower orders." Peasants, shop-keepers, domestic servants—you never open your lips to them without being quite sure of a courteous reply. It costs nothing—cynics may say it means nothing; but, undoubtedly, it is agreeable at the time. For instance, I am accustomed to be on excellent terms with my friends' servants—especially their gardeners. I could name half a dozen in England and Scotland whom I regard as personal friends, and consider an hour spent in their company both agreeable and instructive. But I call to mind a certain Norman *jardinier*, whose first bow of salutation from the cabbage-bed, his "*Pardon, Madame,*" as he proceeded to correct wrong information concerning cider-apples, and his general style of conversation and deportment, were of a kind which inclined one to doubt whether one was talking to "Jean," or "Louis," or to some ancient knight about whom lingered all the courtesies of chivalry. Now I know my friends Duncan or Thomas to be first-rate gardeners and excellent men, and, as I say, I like their company exceedingly; nor would I alter, if I could, any thing about them, their grave, respectful behavior, and honest countenances, lighting up with a demure satisfaction when we sympathize on the subject of a particular flower. Still, I can also admire the charming politeness of my French friends of similar rank; and I think it would not be the worse for either Duncan or Thomas if they were to bring up their children in the doctrine that a little "manners"—that is, a pleasant smile and kindly word to all comers—do neither a poor man nor a rich man any harm.

But, at this rate of proceeding, I shall never quit Caen and its inhabitants, in whom we begun to take a lively interest, and of whom—though we did not know a soul—we have carried away several mute mental photographs, vivid as life, especially an old lady and gentleman in an ancient phaeton, which stopped beside us as we sat under some chestnut-trees in front of the Lycée: he got out, and she sat waiting, reins in hand, for a quarter of an hour or so, looking meditatively out over her pony's ears. How we speculated about her! what sort of life she led at home—I beg pardon, *chez elle;* whether she had children and grandchildren; and if this old French couple were as cosy together as some elderly English couples we had known—which facts we shall never elucidate in this world. Then there was another old man—a very poor-looking, shabby old fellow—who, on being asked if the Musée was open, answered us with the sweetest politeness, walked with us to the door, and took much vain trouble to get us admitted there, finally bidding us a regretful adieu, and lifting his greasy hat with an air worthy of poor old Beau Brummel, who died in a lunatic asylum in this very town of Caen. And there was a young man—a sort of verger in the Church of St. Etienne—who, in our several visits there, showed us the civilest attentions—even politely looking another way when he found us eating biscuits in the sacristy, and showing us, confidentially, all the decorations in preparation for the approaching *Mois de Marie*—which decorations he evidently thought very splendid, and we would not wound his feelings by hinting that these calico draperies and paper roses contrasted strangely with the sombre-vaulted arches of one of the finest churches in France.

But our most curious glimpse of Caen life was a wedding. Once, entering the Church of St. Pierre, which we did about three times a day, we saw, in front of the high altar, a group, evidently intending to be married. They seemed of the *bourgeois* class, but highly respectable: the bride's dress of black silk, with a Lyons shawl, and a white bonnet, was tasteful and good; so was the bridesmaid's; but neither of the young women were at all pretty. However, they both looked gentle, good, and in earnest. For the bridegroom, and two young men who accompanied him, three more ill-looking fellows I have not seen. During the service, which was conducted by one priest and a boy, and seemed much like the ordinary celebration of the mass, with its mutterings, bowings, and so on, these men conducted themselves in a fashion so irreverent as to be scarcely decent. The two groomsmen kept on playing tricks with a long piece of embroidered stuff, something like a hearth-rug, which it seemed part of the ceremony to hold over the heads of the young couple, dropping it down on the bride's dainty bonnet, and ruffling the bridegroom's perfectly-arranged hair, till he turned round quite crossly, and then laughed outright. All this while the plain little bride, whom he scarcely glanced at, knelt meekly by his side; then—the ceremony over—rose and took his arm, tied to him for life. Poor thing! The bridesmaid looked at her, and cried a little—the only person who seemed affected at all. It was an ugly side of French social life, and we went out of the church both sad and angry.

Outside we met the priest, who had hastily put off his magnificent lace—oh! what a flounce for a dinner-dress it would have made!—and in shovel hat and cassock appeared a pleasant gentleman enough — really a gentleman, as was shown by the way in which he stopped to speak to a poor woman with two children, and, stooping down, kissed the little ones so kindly, that we forgave him on the spot for all his necessary mummeries within the church. Possibly he wished to follow in the steps of the late *curé* of St. Pierre, who had died three years before, and whose monument bore two inscriptions—one in French, telling simply the story of his long and virtuous life; the other in Latin, setting forth how, in reward of this, it had pleased his Holiness the Pope to command free exit out of Purgatory for the soul of M. de Montargis. Strange mixture of sense and nonsense, which struck us continually in this Catholic church—the church of a whole nation—nay, of nations; so noble in many of its acts, yet in its beliefs so puerile, that one wonders how any body but children can be got to credit them for a moment.

This was exemplified to us in the *Abbaye aux Dames*, where we went with a vague notion that there, being the eve of May, we should find something interesting going on concerning the Virgin Mary. And, sure enough, we found decking her altar the sweetest-faced elderly nun! —evidently one of the *Dames*, the sisterhood established by Queen Matilda, which now has settled into a convent of forty nuns, who devote themselves to the management of the Hôtel Dieu, or public hospital. She had come laden with white flowers, either in nosegays or pots, and a mass of evergreens, for the adornment of this altar, upon which sat a plaster Mary, about eighteen inches high; such a figure as an Italian image-boy would sell for about half a crown. In lifting it down, a piece of the plaster fell off. "*Ah, c'est cassée—c'est cassée!*" cried the poor nun, in despair. "*Et c'est jolie—si jolie, n'est ce pas?*" added she, turning appealingly to me for sympathy—not in vain. Indeed, I grieve to confess that, but for sterner authority, this recalcitrant Protestant would have bought ever so many white azaleas and ten-week stocks in order to make pretty again that broken Virgin and console the gentle old nun. But she did not lament long; for a young priest came to the rescue, and carried off the figure into the sacristy to mend it—successfully I believe, for next morning I saw my Virgin again—"*your* Virgin Mary!" as she was henceforth satirically termed by stanch Presbyterianism—sitting uninjured in a very bower of white blossoms, no doubt to be worshiped admiringly by the whole of Caen during this month of May, especially consecrated to her.

Strange it is to think what puerile follies, what heathen ceremonials have grown into this worship of Mary! If she, the holy maiden of David's line, the carpenter's wife of Nazareth, the deeply suffering, righteous mother of the Lord Jesus—if she could look down, not as queen of heaven, but as a mortal woman, whose spirit has long gone into peace, to the abode of "those just souls and true" who await the final resurrection, how would she feel? Thinking of her thus—any woman would—I scout the Presbyterian iconoclast, and keep a tender corner in my heart still for "my Virgin Mary."

We were that day leaving Caen, having gone over the town till we had become quite familiar with its churches and streets, its innocent shops, and its curious old houses, where no doubt dwelt many an old Caen family, about whom we used to speculate amusingly as we peeped through the great gates into their court-yards, or their antique gardens full of flowery shrubs, and adorned with that queer flashing crystal ball which the French seem to think such a becoming part of horticultural embellishment. Also, we had driven some miles without the town, seen the stone-quarries, and looked over the uninteresting levels of land, brightened only by great patches of yellow; acres upon acres of the colza plant, whence is produced the colza oil. And we had investigated the broad, smooth, rather dull river, the Orne, with its handsome quays, besides being specially amused by its boat of *blanchisseuses*, where, amidst much chattering and laughing, the garments of the whole town are rinsed, in a most dangerous manner, in the open current of the stream. Finally, we had wandered to the Caen racecourse, where were building all sorts of booths in preparation for the yearly fair, which convinced us that giants and dwarfs, two-headed lambs, and extraordinarily fat babies, nay, even a French edition of Cheap Jack and his wares, were as popular with our neighbors as with ourselves.

In short, there was little more to be seen during the three hours that yet remained to us, so we wandered from the door of the *Abbaye aux Dames* into that of the Hôtel Dieu, the hospital of the sisterhood. Here a small boy—whom I had noticed as being so attentive to his prayers in the church that I asked if he meant to be a priest, at which he shook his pretty head with a gentle

"*Je ne sais—je ne sais rien*"—came up to us, and asked if he should take us to "*les sœurs.*" So with great pride he introduced us to one of them, sitting as portress of the convent, and she consigned us to a sort of lay-sister or servant there, a pleasant-looking, intelligent woman, who showed us every thing without much talking.

A sad sight it was—all hospitals are—yet this had less sadness than most. All was in such exquisite order—white, clean, airy, quiet; the windows looking out on a park green and lovely as that of any palace, where the May sunshine fell, and the new-budded trees rustled merrily, as if sickness and death were unknown in the world. We had hesitations, but our conductress had none, either in the men or women's wards; she took us right through them all, we trying neither to see nor be seen by those sad sickly faces on the pillows, who were being made "comfortable" after the weary night. The *dames*, we heard, watch them sedulously night and day; one *dame*, sixty years old, had been up all last night, and for fourteen nights before that. The whole hospital is under the care of these ladies, most of whom are of good birth, and bring to their establishment their *dot*, whatever it may amount to.

I asked our guide if she knew any thing of another establishment, the *Petites Sœurs des Pauvres*, of which I had heard much. It was begun about ten years ago by one Jeanne Juzan, a servant-maid of Brittany, and it now numbers a hundred and one *maisons*, and maintains from its funds sixteen hundred *sœurs*. These are paid a small yearly sum, about sixteen pounds altogether, and on that they have to live entirely, feed and clothe themselves, without the slightest appeal to charity. "In truth," said my informant, "it is sometimes quite painful when one of the *petites sœurs* will walk over to me, miles across the country, to ask alms for some poor patient she is tending; but as for herself, I am not allowed to give her any thing but a cup of water. How they contrive to live is a marvel, but they do live on their sixteen pounds a year, and can help others likewise."

Their head *maison* in this district is at Caen, so the woman knew all about them, and spoke very highly of them. "But," she said, "the *petites sœurs* are different from our *dames*. They are free to go and come; they see a great deal of the world. But for our *dames* it is *toute autre chose*—quite another thing. When once they enter here, *elles ne sortent plus*."

After that we went into the children's portion of the hospital, a cheerful room, where several small patients were gradually recovering and beginning to play about; and one—well, its pinched, yellow, suffering little face would be very still and sweet, I think, in an hour or two more. A nun with a kind, sad, almost motherly face sat watching it until the end. Then we crossed a field where splendid cows were feeding, to the *Labyrinthe*, a green knoll planted with shrubs, looking over miles of country. Close by was the kitchen-garden, where an elderly nun was walking in the sun; and another garden, quite green, without a single head-stone, only the cross over the entrance-gate, where, the attendant showed us, another nameless hillock had a week ago been made. All was so fresh, so smiling, so lovely, the sweetest place to live in or to die in; yet at every step I seemed to hear the words "*Elles ne sortent plus.*"

Alas! a similar knell rings through many a human life. Fate continually shuts upon us some door which is never opened more. But to shut it of one's own accord, to enter voluntarily a threshold which one knew one should never cross again except into the house appointed for all living, would be a horrible thing. Better all the chances and changes, the struggles and weariness of an existence—in the world, but not of it—whereof the sweets are plain to be seen, and easy to be acknowledged, while the bitternesses lie between ourselves and God—far better all this than the total stagnation, the maddening imprisonment of a haven of rest of which the motto was "*Elles ne sortent plus.*"

We bade adieu to Caen—sweet, pleasant town, which for us will always seem to lie in the sunshine in which we left it—and took our *billets de voyage* for Rouen from a very courteous and elegant young lady appointed to that task. Much it amazed us to see continually on French railways these female officials, down to signal-women and points-women, who at country stations stood, flag in hand, solemnly attentive to duty, and perhaps doing it as well as most men. Undoubtedly French women of all classes have in one thing far more common sense than ours—they know how to work, and they are not ashamed of working. They do not fold their hands in genteel dependence upon fathers, brothers, and husbands—they help them whenever they can. Nor does society consider such help a disgrace to either side. Madame, the wife of the *boutiquier*, continually presides in her shop in the most energetic, accurate, and, withal, lady-like manner; and I have known refined and educated gentlewomen who managed, and managed admirably, the whole accounts of both family and farm, nor thought themselves lowered by such an occupation. In this, too, we might take a leaf out of our neighbor's book with considerable advantage.

A long, sunshiny, shut-up day in a railway carriage is rather an alarming prospect, unless one is certain of one's fellow-passengers, or has the advantage of having none. We glanced anxiously at ours—an elderly military-looking gentleman and two youths, who probably belonged to the Lycée at Caen. It was eleven o'clock, the universal hour for *déjeûner;* so the three proceeded to regale themselves in the temperate French fashion upon a roll of dry bread a piece, and then began to chat, and joke, and play together in the most lively way. And here we could not help noticing—what, indeed, struck us wherever we went in France—the extremely free relations that exist between parents and children. In England, and especially in Scotland, however deep and tender the love, there is always a certain distance kept up. Now these lads played tricks with their father that would have made a British parent's hair stand on end with horror, fondling over him the while with a kind of rough caressing that was queer, certainly, to us undemonstrative islanders; yet he seemed to like it, and to be used to it. This was, perhaps, an exceptional case; they might have been the spoiled children of his old age; but among all French children we noticed toward their elders, both in speech and manner, a sweet, frank liberty, which never degenerated into license. Throughout France "the nursery" is only a room for the babies; as soon as the little folk can toddle about or wield a knife and fork, they are admitted freely both to the *salon* and the *salle à manger*, and share the occupations and amusements of the family in a manner that with us is quite unknown. Possibly, with some natures, this may have its disadvantages—making them men and women too soon; but it certainly makes them little gentlemen and gentlewomen, and it saves them entirely from that mixture of shyness and underbredness which is sometimes seen, for a time, in very good and sweet children who have been kept continually in their nurseries, and accustomed to associate chiefly with servants.

For instance, when our Caen fellow-travelers left us, they were succeeded by a carriageful of children—rather rough-looking boys, and a big *gauche* girl—in charge of an elderly person, who might be a *bonne*, an aunt, or a grandmother. We soon discovered that she was the latter, and that these were four orphans of whom she had the bringing-up—rather a heavy handful for one so well advanced in years. The lads, excited by their journey, were just a little noisy; but their fun never once degenerated in naughtiness, and a grave shake of the head or a gentle "*Soyez sage, mes petits,*" was the utmost reproof they ever obtained or deserved. Certainly they chattered incessantly, and amused themselves in the most independent way, perfectly at their ease both as regarded their grandmother and us; but the heaviest sin they committed was a very venial one, namely, writing on their slates and passing round to one another certain written comments on *ces Anglais;* which, after having discovered that French was not an unknown tongue to us, they

—children as they were—were too polite to make aloud in the vernacular.

After they left us—leaping out into the arms of a Norman peasant and peasant woman, who suddenly came from a farm close by the station, and who greeted them with an eagerness of affection quite charming to see—the little people still did not forget, as the train moved off, to watch for the passing of our carriage, and lift their caps to us in a farewell salutation, as "*sage*" as the good grandmother could possibly have desired. Indeed, we should rather have missed their company had we not been just then passing into a country that was really interesting — the forest-country between Bourgtheronde and Rouen.

For many miles that line of railway skirts two enormous forests—the Forêt de la Londe and the Forêt de Rouvray; in the latter of which William the Conqueror is said to have been hunting when he heard of the death of Edward the Confessor and the seizure of the English crown by Harold. It is a very wild forest still, and appeared to us almost entirely uninhabited. Sometimes for miles we sped along between two sloping uplands of underwood, with not even a cart-track or footpath visible, and occasionally we saw glades desolate and lovely as those in the New Forest of Hampshire. But the days of wild beasts are past, and probably there are neither bears nor wolves to be hunted, though I can not say for certain. Once, in Normandy, we really did hear of a wolf—a she-wolf and her cubs—being seen in a wood not many miles off; but as it was from the lips of imaginative childhood, we do not wish to vouch too strongly for the fact. Still, that in very hard winters wolves do come down from the mountains and desolate the farms, is undeniable.

At Elbœuf we crossed the Seine, now grown into a fine broad river with magnificent banks—great chalk cliffs, broken into all sorts of curious shapes, called Les Rochers d'Orival. While waiting at the station, in the way that French trains seem to have a trick of doing, just for amusement, we had a fine view of these rocks, dyed in faint colors by the sinking sun. And all the way to Rouen, the Seine, winding in and out, was a beautiful bright object. We were grieved to lose sight of it, and creep into civilization through an array of bricks and mortar, ominously reminding us of Manchester or Birmingham.

I suppose I had unconsciously connected Rouen with mediæval romance, Joan of Arc, and so forth; but I certainly had not expected to find it a big, modern, manufacturing town, approached through mills and warehouses, its streets being gradually rebuilt into painful newness—a second Paris, in short. And our inn—which, not having to speak well of, I will not name—what a contrast it was to the quiet little hostelry at Caen, where we were served so well, and made so "comfortable," according to the word we expressed at parting, and which was the only bit of English our beaming landlady seemed to comprehend! The *table d'hôte*, also, with its frantic attempts at English cooking, administered in French quantities, its sanguine *gigots*, and intolerable *poudings*, was trying to hungry travelers. It was in rather a depressed frame of mind that we issued out to see the town; that is, the churches, for we went straight to the Cathedral, of course.

It is said to be of inferior architecture—florid and tasteless; certainly its ornamentation outside is lavish to redundancy; yet there was a charm in its multitude of saints and angels, stuck in every available niche, and every one of which must have been the workmanship of some skillful and careful hand, now long forgotten. There is to me something pathetic in the individualism of this mediæval architecture—the lingering labor of years, completed with a personal devotedness, which in our rapid machinery-days we can scarcely comprehend. We smile at stories like that of Alexander Berneval, the master-mason of St. Ouen, who slew his apprentice for surpassing himself in a rose-window, and was accordingly most justly hanged; only the monks, considering what a beautiful church he had built for them, allowed his body to be buried within it. Such things seem impossible now—as impossible as it is to believe in the insanities perpetrated by Huguenots and Revolutionists in this very cathedral—bonfires lit in the nave to burn priests' vestments and melt down sacramental plate; tombs broken open, and the bodies of good men, who had slept there for centuries, scattered abroad.

Let us hope that the world has outgrown such childish wickedness, and only perpetrates childish follies, such as we witnessed on going suddenly out of the dim nave into the lighted choir. There we saw a grand altar, decked out with yards upon yards of coarse white muslin and stiff calico roses, after the fashion of a county ballroom, interspersed with flowers half real, half artificial, or both mixed together, in that kind of taste which belongs to Catholic church decorations—which, in such a proverbially tasteful people as the French, I can only characterize as being at once most surprising and most abominable. About the whole were stuck myriads of wax candles of different sizes, and so numerous that it took a boy with a long stick a full half hour to light them all.

In front of this show we found slowly collecting a large congregation, of which a good proportion were children, who seemed highly interested and delighted; and no wonder, for the sight was as pretty as a Christmas-tree, or an exhibition of fireworks. Finally, a girls' school, under charge of half a dozen nuns, was marched up, an organist seated himself at a harmonium close by, and the service began. It consisted of prayers—in French, not in Latin; a sort of litany, in the responses to which all joined; a hymn, simple and sweet, and sung excellently by the children and nuns; and a sermon, also in French—a very good moral discourse by an elderly priest. Again there was a long hymn, one of those half-cheerful, half-plaintive tunes which are used as litanies to the Virgin; and then, about nine o'clock, the congregation dispersed.

A most innocent service, which we were told would take place here every evening during the *Mois de Marie*. In it, as usual, we noticed the extreme earnestness of the worshipers, and the large proportion of the very poor among them. One young woman, who brought a two-year-old baby in her arms, held it in front of her, with its little hands folded between hers, and its round eyes staring at the dazzle of lights, for a full quarter of an hour, while she remained kneeling upon the bare marble floor, absorbed in devotion. And there sat close beside me half a dozen boys of the roughest age and lowest order of boy-kind, who came in by themselves, and, though there was no beadle to box their ears, behaved in a manner that I could wish was imitated by every Sunday-school scholar of my acquaintance.

We went "home" (as we persisted in saying every where—and perhaps there was a deep truth in the word) to our inn, finding nothing particularly interesting in the Rouen streets. They seemed merely an imitation of Paris—as indeed the whole town did—until, next morning, we suddenly passed out of its glaring sunshine in at the little church door of St. Ouen.

After a certain course of churches, one church gets to look very much like another, at least to us who possess no architectural learning to teach the difference between them. But it is the peculiarity of the highest class of Art that we feel it without understanding it—it appeals to ignorant as well as to enlightened appreciations. Therefore, though I can not in the least explain why, St. Ouen stands out in my memory as the most beautiful of all the churches we saw—a real temple, full of that beauty, visible and spiritual, which is the combined result of the most perfect skill. I can still shut my eyes and think I stand at our favorite point of view, just in front of the high altar—looking east—on those lofty avenues that melt upward into a dim blue haze like the sky itself for peace; and to right and left are those exquisite rose-windows, the peculiar but delicious harmonies of which give one, in color, the sensation I have sometimes felt in sound, as if a piece of music were at once perfectly new, and yet perfectly familiar, having been heard before in a previous existence.

St. Ouen was our chief delight; we went in and out of it—I smile to think how often. Still, we "did" Rouen valorously, even down to the Hôtel de Ville, with its atrocious pictures distributed through the most charming of galleries, its ancient streets, its market-place where Jeanne de la Pucelle was burnt; nay, we conscientiously put ourselves in charge of a sleepy horse and drowsier driver, who, being roused up periodically, only answered with the calmest politeness, "*Oui, oui, madame, j'aime beaucoup dormir,*" and at length found ourselves on the summit of the hill where has been lately built the chapel of *Notre Dame de Bon Secours;* a most beautiful chapel after the modern style of ornamentation, not unlike the newly-restored crypt in our Westminster Hall, with an altar the richest we have yet seen. Here, too, there was some taste shown—not mere decorative upholstery and formal flowers stuck into common little china pots, but wreaths of evergreens, tall white lilies, and white azaleas, arranged with a lovingness befitting the devotion of a good Catholic to Mary in the month of May. On either side, extending down the wall of the chapel, were votive tablets in white marble, bearing curious inscriptions, some quite anonymous, some marked with a name or initials, but all breathing devout gratitude, and telling, or implying, stories so touching that one could not laugh at them even when they verged on the ridiculous. For instance, a lady inscribed—in most colloquial French—how her faithful man-servant fell ill on a journey of typhus fever, and after divers remedies, minutely stated, had all failed, she prayed to *Notre Dame de Bon Secours*, and the man immediately recovered. Some of these votive inscriptions were mere outbursts of thankfulness—"*Marie, mon Secours;*" "*Honneur à Marie;*" "*J'ai prié Marie, et elle a exaucée ma prière;*" "*Ma fille était moribonde, et Marie l'a donnée à mon amour;*" or else a mere date, with the motto "*Grâces à Marie;*" or two dates, with "*Marie m'a écoutée deux fois.*"

Very strange they were, these half revelations of many a secret, these records of many a gone-by sorrow. No doubt some good people would have turned from them as blasphemous, horrible; but to us they seemed only pitiful—an accidental leaf out of the great chronicle of human woe, which will never be closed until the world's end; touching, too, as being instances of thankfulness—cries of joy arising from the vast suffering multitude, to one half of whom comes no relief to be thankful for, while the other half seldom acknowledge it when it comes. Alas! these poor blind souls acknowledged it amiss; still, the gratitude was there, and perhaps He who is the giver of all good things would not wholly despise the full heart, though it poured itself out only to the Virgin Mary.

From the chapel we went out on the hill-side to the little cemetery, the graves of which overlook—strange phrase concerning that silent, sightless company!—a view as extensive as it is magnificent. The whole valley of the Seine, from Rouen almost to Elbœuf, lies spread out as in a map, and on this clear day, with only a few white spring clouds floating over the bluest of skies, it was lovely—a bit of earth that makes one seem to understand heaven—a sight that, in spite of these graves and many more, taught us that *le bon Dieu* was Himself still. And though there is no *Notre Dame de Bon Secours*, no pitiful Virgin Mary from whom help might be implored, no votive shrine at which could be bought immunity from sickness and sorrow—though, God knows! many a prayer goes up blankly to Him, and falls down again, unanswered, upon bleeding hearts and new-filled tombs—alas! we had heard of some that day—yet through it all He is there. Close at hand night and day; with us, as with His natural world, working darkly on in His own way; ready finally to work out even death itself, which seems the greatest evil, into the most perfect good. How, we know not; but there are days, and this was one of them, when, without knowing, we can believe.

Among other things at Rouen we had been charged to visit the Musée des Antiquités, where we found many curiosities—none more so than the old curator. How polite he was, the funny little old man! how eager about his stained glass and his fragments of Gothic architecture! What a deal of information he gave us, condescendingly, in broken French, which he probably thought would be more intelligible to foreigners! I am afraid we were not learned enough for him, as the principal thing we noticed was a headless, draped statue—apparently a portrait statue—which had been dug out of some ancient baths. Charming beyond any thing that we had seen for long was the simple grace of this young Roman maiden, done in marble for later centuries to gaze at and speculate over—not idealized at all; just a girl in her girlish clothing, as her mother might have dressed her, yet it put the ideal quite to shame—or, rather, it was the ideal, as the real often is unawares—this common every-day life, which time will translate into history and poetry—a creed evidently not that of our friend the curator; for when, after he had shown us all sorts of queer things—of course all ancient—ending with a handful of brown dust, kept under glass, said to be the veritable " lion" heart of Richard Cœur de Lion, we asked a meek question about a very good modern bust close by, he answered carelessly, "*Oh, c'est un Monsieur;*" adding, with the utmost disdain, "*Il vit encore.*" Hapless gentleman!

We spent the evening on the bridges and quays, watching the sun set down the broad Seine, and noting the passers-by, of whom, as usual, about a third seemed to be soldiers. Never was there such a country for soldiers! In Paris, one can not walk about for half an hour without meeting several detachments of them filing down the streets, either with music or without. I wonder if it is done on the same principle that I encourage my cats in the free range of the house, not necessarily to eat the mice, but only to frighten them!

Next morning, we spent our last few hours at Rouen in taking a farewell round of the churches, ending at St. Godard, where we came in for one more glimpse of French life—another marriage; but quite different from that of Caen: here, from the carpet spread on the church steps to the poetical-looking young organist who discoursed soft music during the whole ceremony, all was elegant and aristocratic. So was the company; and dressed—oh, Fashion! what enormities do even the tasteful French nation perpetrate in thy name! Never, in the richest and roughest of English or Scotch manufacturing towns, did I see such bonnets, mounted upon such heaps of impossibly luxuriant hair, and exhibiting bold and bare faces — well, we are not accountable for our own faces, but we are for the manner in which we display them obnoxiously to our neighbors. Would that these good, plain, large-visaged elderly ladies could understand how a little reticence—a little retirement beneath soft blonde and neat ribbons, will often make even an ugly person tolerable to beholders. But it is vain to preach. At least we had the consolation of finding that our Gallic neighbors were as silly as ourselves—

Except the bride. She was scarcely at all pretty, and yet it was a pleasure to look upon her, from the excessive simplicity of her dress. Her high white gown—of silk or satin, I forget which—fitted her perfectly, and fell down in pure pre-Raffaelite folds; her orange-wreath was set neatly upon her smooth hair, and her veil of white tulle covered her down to her feet. This charming costume, added to her extreme youth, and the grave, decorous behavior of both herself and her young bridegroom, made them a pretty sight to behold as they knelt in the sunshine before the high altar. The ceremony was long (apparently it took more trouble, and more priests, to marry these "genteel" people than our *bourgeois* friends at Caen), and a good deal of it consisted in applications to the purse of bride or bridegroom; six times at least I saw them giving alms.

As we sat looking at this young couple, guessing about

their past, and speculating on what their future might be—concerning neither of which we are ever likely to learn any thing—they reminded us tenderly of a similar ceremony which was that very day and hour being celebrated in a certain English chapel we knew. We kept wondering how all had "gone off" there; how every body behaved and looked—the dear familiar faces; some very lovely, and all so good, and sweet, and kind. Thinking of them, this young "Flore" and "Victor Eugène"—we caught their Christian names, though of all else concerning them we are, and shall ever remain, in profoundest ignorance—became more interesting. We watched them, I confess, with somewhat dimmed eyes; nor will it harm them, whoever they be, that the two heretics, on quitting the church, left a hearty, silent blessing behind.

Another of those long and slow railway journeys, which incline us to believe that the French are the most patient, or we the most impatient of races, and toward evening we found ourselves at Amiens, with, alas! one of our *malles* a-missing—a box that, under the unimportant bonnet, contained books and papers of quite peculiar value. Great was the grief feminine, and loud the masculine reprobation of every thing French, especially the French system of *bagages*. A knot of sympathizing porters gathered round, and one of them fetched the *chef de la gare*—viz., station-master, whose courtesy was overwhelming.

"It was most unfortunate; such a thing hardly ever happened. But Madame might make herself quite easy; the box must be found. Was it of *fer, bois, cuir?*" and he indicated some of each sort. But in the confusion the French word for tin had unluckily escaped both our memories, and description failed. Some one conceived the bright thought of producing a dictionary. The *chef* seized it, and began searching in the most urbane manner for the word which he could not possibly know. At last, just as we had made the blessed discovery, *étain*, appeared three porters, beaming with triumph, carrying three boxes, one being actually the right one. "I told Madame it was sure to be found," observed the smiling official, and with another series of bows he retired, followed by the band of porters, who not one of them made the slightest suggestion of an eleemosynary franc. We Britons, our grief healed, our anger mollified, stood meek as lambs, and beg to record gratefully the incident, as being the only difficulty we met with in all our journeyings.

These were now drawing to a close. This sunset, which shone so pleasantly in the hôtel garden, and lighted up the old cathedral towers, would be our last in France. No more churches to wander in and out of, no more lazy sauntering down evening streets, watching the humors of the crowd, in that excellent holiday idleness which only hard-working people can fully appreciate. As we pushed open the heavy double doors of Amiens Cathedral, and thought that this was our last French church for at least a long time, we were just a little dull.

It was nearly eight o'clock, and already the evening mists had began to float high up among the aerial arches, and hide from us the painted windows, chapels, and tombs. Still we saw as much as we could, under the guidance of the young *huissier*, or beadle, or something, who seemed excessively proud of his cathedral, and who asked if we would not like to "assist" in the service just beginning? We assenting, he found us seats where we could watch a large congregation slowly gather between the choir and the nave, in front of the altar to the Virgin.

It was the finest and prettiest decked altar we had yet seen. Behind it was a large shield or screen, adorned with mottoed scrolls, on which was inscribed "*Mater purissima,*" "*Virgo Beata,*" "*Stella Maris,*" "*Regina Cœlorum*"—every conceivable epithet that Catholic devotion bestows on the mother of Christ. Above it, white, life-sized, and gracefully sculptured, she sat, with her child in her arms, in that wonderful peace, beauty, and benignity of motherhood, which, as represented in some of these Catholic churches, must touch the very stoniest of Protestant hearts. When the myriad wax candles, which took about three quarters of an hour to light, were all lit, the effect was marvelous. You could almost fancy, in the flicker of the illumination, that you saw the mother softly smile, or that the child moved its little arms, and extended them over the multitude. And all the while the sweet monotonous litany, sung now by deep male voices, rose and fell, and its steady response— "*Ora pro nobis,*" I think it was—came back and back like the beating of a wave against the shore.

Then, making his way with difficulty through the enormous congregation, which spread itself in darkness far down the nave, came a priest, sprinkling us all from a wet brush on either side. All clean water is holy water, so why object? It did us no harm; nor did the sermon, which was a remarkably fine piece of oratory, very dramatic, very French, delivered by a priest with a voice as musically sonorous as that of Mr. Spurgeon himself. The subject was that of strayed sheep; how families are broken up, parents' gray hairs dishonored, and young lives wrecked—more lives than that of the poor sinner, and for what? that he may enjoy the pleasures of sin for a season—a season so very brief. Nothing novel, but eloquently and vividly put, after the Spurgeon manner, though with much more refinement. Only, what would that popular preacher have said, could he have seen this other popular preacher, who in many things much resembled himself, when, suddenly turning round to the altar, blazing with light, and the white figure sitting above it, the priest clasped his hands theatrically, and exclaiming *"Sainte Vierge!"* began a passionate invocation to Mary, calling upon her to behold, and pity, and take away all these sins, all these sorrows?—a cry which might have been partly in earnest—it did not appear so, but let us give the preacher the benefit of the doubt. The sermon was listened to with an earnestness dumb as death by the entire congregation. But oh! when one looked round at them, these poor sheep of the wilderness, as one does at many another similar multitude in our own land, seeking food and finding—what? one could imagine how the heart of the great Shepherd must yearn over them—His still—wherever they are. And one clung to the belief—the hope at least—that He may all the while be leading them home by many a path that we know nothing of, though we think in our blindness we know every thing that there is to be known.

When the discourse was over came a long hushed pause,

and then there rose up from behind the screen a cloud of clear treble voices, singing in two parts, first and second, a tune very familiar in many of our modern English churches, and generally adapted to one of the most beautiful of our modern hymns—Keble's "Sun of my Soul." Though we knew it was only a litany to the Virgin, which these poor people of Amiens were hymning to that white figure, so sweet and saintly that we almost forgave them for imagining it divine, still we could not help lingering and singing it with them, not in Latin, but in the words of the good old man not long departed:

> "Sun of my soul, Thou Savior dear,
> It is not night if Thou be near;
> Oh may no earth-born cloud arise
> To hide Thee from Thy servant's eyes.
>
> Abide with me from morn till eve,
> For without Thee I can not live:
> Abide with me when night is nigh,
> For without Thee I dare not die.
>
> Thou, Framer of the light and dark,
> Steer through the tempest Thine own ark!
> Amid the howling wintry sea,
> We are in port if we have Thee.
>
> Come near and bless us when we wake,
> Ere through this world our way we take;
> Till, in the ocean of Thy love,
> We lose ourselves in heaven above."

And then, mingling silently with the unknown crowd—unknown to us as we to them, but every one alike children of the Father in heaven—we quitted Amiens Cathedral.

Sixteen hours after we were standing on English

shores, and hearing around us English voices. *La belle France* was nothing but a dream.

But, such as it was, I have set it down—a mere glimpse at best; yet I am sure, if I "nothing extenuate," I "set down naught in malice." There may be many things seen *couleur de rose* which a nearer view would paint much darker; and yet I am not ashamed of that: a surface judgment is daring indeed if it presumes to be other than a pleasant one. And other things may have been said incorrectly or judged amiss, but I trust nothing has been judged unconscientiously or said unkindly. For us, the travelers, we went in the true traveling spirit, to observe rather than to criticise; to learn rather than to teach. And we *have* learnt—much that is never likely to be forgotten by us to the end of our days.

CHAPTER III.

A CITY AT PLAY.

"*Les Anglais n'aiment pas s'amuser, n'est-ce pas, Madame?*"

This remark (which at once removed any pleasing delusion as to my own French that her amiable reception of it might have caused) was made to me one clear, cold spring day, nearly a year after our first appearance in *la belle France*, and when we had just crossed the Channel for an idle week—not in France provincial, but in its metropolis; we wished, in short, to "see Paris." My interlocutor was a respectable middle-aged Parisienne, of the *bourgeois* class, perhaps a little below it—for she wore no bonnet, but one of those snowy white caps which no English laundress could hope to rival. She and I stood together, clinging to the railings of the high walk which bounds the Jardin des Tuileries, and looking down the Rue de Rivoli toward the Place de la Concorde, across which the Procession of *le Bœuf Gras* was to pass. For this was the second of the three days of Carnival; and though it was still *grand matin*—not much past nine A.M.—and the sharp east wind shook angrily the black trees behind us, and there was not a ray of sunshine even in sunshiny Paris, nevertheless all the Parisian world and his wife, and especially all their children, were abroad—"*pour s'amuser.*"

Of course, business still went on down the Rue de Rivoli, at least in the centre of it. There were the usual heavy country carts drawn by white Norman horses, queerly caparisoned, driven by blue-bloused peasants, who looked as if they had never been in Paris before; the lumbering omnibuses, also with white horses (I think nine tenths of the French horses are either white or gray); the incessant *remises* and *fiacres*, and the occasional carriages. But down each side of the street flowed a continual stream of people—apparently idle people. At every convenient corner they gathered into groups, and all along the Tuileries railings they hung in a row, like pins stuck on a pin-paper, wedged as close as possible.

I had tried to be polite to my right-hand neighbor, but she was grumpy—the only grumpy Frenchwoman I ever met. Perhaps she thought herself in too low company, for she was a shade higher in rank than my left-hand friend: she wore a bonnet, and a velvet one too. My meek attempts at conversation she altogether snubbed, and when I dared to borrow a hand-bill she carried—a *Promenade du Bœuf Gras*, with a description (my own had none)—and began copying it in pencil on my knees, she eyed me with exceeding distrust, as if I were plotting something against the state. With her imposing size—she was decidedly fat—she contrived to render my footing so insecure that I certainly should have slipped down from the railings had it not been for my good-natured friend on the other side, the *bourgeoise* aforesaid.

Consequently, the good woman and I entered into sociable conversation about the *Bœuf Gras*, the coming procession, and the Carnival in general, which, I had heard, was expected to be particularly good this year.

My neighbor shook her head: "Ah! if Madame had seen it, as I remember it, twenty years ago!" And she kept repeating the words "*il y a vingt ans*" with a lingering emphasis; then burst into a voluble description of what the Paris Carnival was then, in the midst suddenly making the remark with which I have began this paper.

I quite agreed with her in the opinion concerning our nation, but said, laughing, that some hereditary French blood made me an exception to the rule, and, though I was an Englishwoman, I very much liked to—but how shall I translate that quite untranslatable verb *s'amuser?* It does not mean "to be amused," that is, by other people—the dreariest sort of amusement I know; still less does it imply "to amuse one's self" in a solitary, selfish spirit. I take it to express most nearly the occupation of children at play, not bent upon any special entertainment, but simply catching the humor of the moment; snatching the present as it flies, and looking neither behind nor before. A condition of mind not only harmless, but often excellently wise, and which my Parisienne was quite right in supposing was with us English only too rare.

Yes, as a nation we certainly do no not care to amuse ourselves. Nothing would ever make any of our cities or towns wear the aspect of that "city at play," such as I saw it during the three days of Carnival. And, descending from the aggregate to the individual in that gay crowd, nothing certainly could have been further from the mind of any middle-aged British matron than to do as the Frenchwoman did—to turn out from her home and her family at nine o'clock on a bleak February morning, and spend an hour or so quite alone, perched like a bird upon a railing, waiting for the passing by of a rather childish show—simply "*pour s'amuser.*"

Yet I neither blame nor praise her; I merely state the fact. It is only on returning to this excellent, rich, hard-working, but just a little too solemn England, that the drop or two of French blood in me—the reference to which my Parisienne received with congratulatory approval—makes me linger with a certain pleasure over a few pictures left by this Carnival city; wishing secretly, perhaps, that there was with us at home a little less work, a little more play—yes, actual play.

It was on Sunday, of course, that the fun began—a true February day, bright and bleak; the sunshine clear, as Paris sunshine always is; the cold biting, intense, as Paris cold well knows how to be; so that crossing the great square of the Louvre made one feel as if one were being kissed and killed in a breath. Now there are elements in a Paris Sunday which will always make it repellant—I will say repulsive—to the British mind. The streets looking just as upon a week-day; work going on as usual, without a sign of the day of rest; the shops universally open, save the very few who boldly mark on their closed shutters "*Fermée le Dimanche.*" No; we can not—I fervently trust we never shall—reconcile ourselves to this total ignoring of Sabbath repose, which, based merely upon human grounds, seems such a vital necessity.

But if the shops are open, so are the churches. Soon after eight A.M. I went in and joined a throng of worshipers, chiefly working people, men and women, who in England would probably have been sleeping off the Saturday night's over-eating or over-drinking in their beds. And, without being in the least inclined to Roman Catholicism, or to that hybrid form of it, Ritualism, I say decidedly, I wish every one of our churches was open every day, and all day long. Undoubtedly, before it began to play, the city said its prayers, and very earnest prayers too. Then, about noon, it turned out in all its best clothes—and the best clothes of a young or even old Parisienne are very different from those of a Cockney—inundating the streets with pretty, suitable, tasteful toilettes. There were very few bonnets, or the apologies for bonnets that women wear now, but in their stead the universal *capuchon*, of violet, scarlet, black, and white, the most becoming head-dress any woman could wear. And the gowns were all decently short—no street-sweeping; while as to the petticoats, their variety was a sight to behold!

I can not say the women were pretty—not even in holiday clothes—but they all looked bright and gay, as holiday-makers should. They came out in twos and threes, pairs of sweethearts, or knots of female companions. There were many domestic groups—the father, mother, and one child; a quiet triad; for children in Paris are not over-numerous, and grave as little old men and women. One misses the constant gush of child-life which overfloods our London in park, street, alley, and square. Instead comes another item of street-population wholly unknown to us—those odd-looking Zouaves, with their queer, sharp brown faces, and dark, wistful eyes, almost like children's eyes, whom one meets every dozen yards or so, wandering vaguely about, like strange creatures newly caught, and not quite naturalized yet.

Such were a few of the elements of this holiday crowd, which began to circulate about, hither and thither, after *le Bœuf Gras;* this *foule immense* (as it is called, with a *naïveté* very foreign to our mural inscriptions, on the base of Cleopatra's Needle, at the Place de la Concorde), which is said to give its rulers so much trouble, because it will insist upon being amused. As a curious confirmation of this, and of the vital difference between the two races, English and French, I was informed by one who had had many years' opportunity of testing the fact, that the Paris Préfet's daily list of criminal accusations was always shorter after a fête-day than at any other time. I am afraid our police-sheet of any given 26th of December, or Easter Tuesday, would not show the same statistics.

Yet a London crowd is a fine sight. The "many-headed monster thing" is rather a noble beast than not. Courageous, self-reliant, well-behaved — generous, too, with a rough sense of justice, and an admiration for "pluck"—a stanch stickler for its own rights, yet not encroaching on those of its neighbor; and having, in the main, that quick sympathy with the good, and contempt for the bad, which is found invariably in large masses of men, as if to prove, in spite of the doctrine of original sin, that the deepest stratum of human nature is not bad, but good. But on its "general holidays," the brightest of them, say a royal marriage or funeral—for both come alike to the too-rare holiday-makers—the British public is a somewhat sullen animal, which takes its pleasures with a solemn rapacity, knowing they are but few, and is rather hard to deal with, tenacious of affront, obnoxious to harsh rule, prone to grumble loudly at its voluntary hardships. Besides, a large proportion of it is not "on pleasure bent" at all, but pursuing its vocation, whether of pocket-picking, seat-letting, or orange and cake selling, with a business-like pertinacity, never turned aside by such a small thing as amusement.

Now this Paris *foule* seems wholly bent on amusing itself. "*Toujours gai*" is its motto, written plainly on its face; and to this end every body is on the best possible terms with every body. No jostling, no scrambling. Its "looped and windowed raggedness" is as civil and even courteous as velvet and lace. "Monsieur" and "Madame" are heard on every side, and the vast multitude is on such excellent terms with itself and every body else that it goes swaying on as easily as a mass of sea-waves.

All this with us is utterly unknown. In a London crowd I should no more have ventured to go about—sometimes alone even—as I did in Paris, than I would have penetrated into the monkeys' cage at the Zoological Gardens. Quite safe, no doubt, but exceedingly uncomfortable. Now here it was more than comfortable—agreeable. The studies of life were endless, whether we let ourselves be floated through the Palais Royal or Rue de Rivoli, or mingled in the thinner crowd which filled like an ever-moving kaleidoscope the Tuileries Gardens, feeding the swans, or looking—no, I fear very few looked —at the sunset. Yet what a sunset it was!—radiant with all the colors of spring; and how it gleamed on the white statues, and lit up in wonderful clearness the long, straight line—perhaps the finest straight line of street in any city—which extends from the palace of the Tuileries up to the Arc de Triomphe.

We left it there—this gay Sunday crowd—and caught it up again, as I stated, on the Monday morning, eager at its pleasures, and waiting with infantile delight for the passing of the celebrated procession of the *Bœuf Gras*.

And here, to show that there is another and a serious hard-working side to this city at play, I will make a divergence.

The show was a very fine show in its way. It was composed of about five hundred people, besides horses. It had six emblematic *chars* descriptive of Europe, Asia, Africa, and America, besides a *Char d'Olympe* filled with gods and goddesses, and a *Char d'Agriculture*, wherein rode the twelve months and the four seasons. All these were dressed in the most classic style, and with, I must say, remarkably good taste. Then there was a huge *char* full of costumed musicians, playing vehemently, and a troop of *cavaliers peaux rouges*, twenty or more, who sat their horses with a skill more belonging to the Hippodrome than to the backwoods of America; while in the midst journeyed the garlanded, gilt-horned victims, the four *bœufs gras—Mignon, le Lutteur masqué, Paul Forestier*, and, lastly, *Gulliver*, a magnificent beast, who, with his huge head tied safely down, kept turning on the throng those large, patient, pathetic ox-eyes. All this procession, which traversed Paris street by street for three days, stopping at the principal public offices and private abodes for royal or noble *largesse*, was under the arrangement and at the expense of a certain M. Duval, a *bourgeois* hero in his way.

In "La Petite Presse" of that date—one of those flaccid journals so limp as to their paper, so florid and grandiose in their style—I found an account of him, which, in its dramatic form of putting things, almost rivaled the *feuilleton* which followed—a tale describing "la prison de *Clarkenweld*" [sic], and the interior of Newgate, in a manner strikingly original. If I remember rightly, the governor, a Sir Somebody Something, is a gentleman of bland manners, always smiling, who, handling his own keys, escorts an amazed Frenchman through Newgate to the condemned cell, which they find fitted up as a mortuary chapel, the soul of the criminal having just departed in an exemplary manner, surrounded by lighted candles and all the last rites of the Catholic Church. (This *par parenthèse*, though it strikes us with an alarming humility, lest our pictures of foreigners should unwittingly be as far from the truth as theirs of ourselves.)

Scarcely less peculiar is the sketch of M. Duval, the "*acquéreur des bœufs gras*," as he terms himself. It is so funny, in its serio-comic sentiment, and its reckless trenching upon what we call in England "the sanctities of private life," that I can not resist translating it entire.

"*Rue de Rome*, numéro 5. Behold us standing opposite to one of those grand mansions whose mere exterior implies wealth and commerce. There lives M. Duval, with his family. There also is his place of business, where he carries on the administration of his vast enterprises, his *bouillons*, laundries, bakers' and butchers' shops, his aquarium, etc., etc. M. Duval is a great capitalist, who loves to employ his capital in many different spheres of action. He possesses an Egeria—his wife, an admirable woman of business, clever alike in advising and in acting. He has a son and heir, twenty years old, qualifying himself by the translating of Livy and Tacitus to preside at his father's slaughter-houses; who now listens to the lowing of Virgil's kine, and studies under Pliny the habits of fish.

"Around Generalissimo Duval gravitates a whole army of *employés;* yearly some new battle-field is won. Now it is a wine and spirit shop newly opened at Berry; again a washing and baking establishment, conducted on the same principle as the world-known *bouillons;* or else it is the great aquarium on the Boulevard Montmartre, which cost its projector 230,000 francs. 'Too much,' said the gossips. M. Duval listened, smiling. During the Exposition of 1867, 250,000 persons visited his fish! This fact shows his success—another will prove how well he deserves it. He found out that his piscine flock would not thrive on shore sea-water; he immediately chartered a Dieppe steamer, and went out into deep sea-water, bringing back to Paris not only quantities of fish, but oceans of their native element.

"M. Duval's best claim to public gratitude is the establishment of his *bouillons économiques*, the noble substitutes for those execrable *gargotes*, familiar to all who have known Paris for the last twenty years, as being the only place where one could get a dinner at from 19 to 25 sous. In their stead—from 1840 to 1845—the Dutch *bouillons* vainly tried to succeed. M. Duval caught the idea, improved upon it, and, beginning at the Rue de la Monnaie, created the twelve establishments which now bear his name.

"At first he only supplied *bouillon* and beef; but soon the bill of fare was extended. The Parisian public fully appreciated these restaurants, where, for the same low price as heretofore, one was excellently served in airy rooms, on marble tables, with well-cooked food of first-rate quality, which one could eat without being poisoned. True, the portions were each rather small; but huge eaters might call for a second portion without ruining themselves. Twenty or thirty sous will procure a capital dinner at the Bouillons Duval.

"Besides, there are no waiters; but waitresses, which gives employment to a number of women. Undoubtedly, one might greatly desire, with Michelet and other political economists, that the wages of the husband and father should always suffice for the family, while the wife sinks into her true place as mother and manager at home. The children's education, and the whole moral life of the household, would gain much thereby. But, alas! facts are against M. Michelet. His theory is but a beautiful dream. Practically, the husband's wages are not sufficient to maintain the family. The wife must work likewise; and those who help her to work—in a feminine way—do much good in their generation. The number of girls and women employed by M. Duval must have benefited many a household.

"Let us visit one of the *bouillons;* take, for instance, the one in the Rue de Rivoli" [where, this present writer solemnly avers, that she and a friend—neither of them "huge eaters," but yet sufficiently and wholesomely hungry with Paris sight-seeing—lunched admirably off meat, potatoes, bread, and maccaroni for the large sum of a franc and a half—say sevenpence halfpenny apiece].

"On entering, we are presented with a printed bill of fare—meats and wines—the price of each plainly marked. We sit down at a table of white marble, adorned with the little equipage of pepper and salt, and the decanter containing clear, cool water, sparkling and fresh. Immediately there comes to us a young woman, neatly dressed in white apron and spotless muslin cap; she takes our orders, and writes upon our *carte* whatever we desire—*potage, bouillon*, meat, vegetables, wine. We are served accurately and rapidly. The plates, knives, and forks are clean and abundant. If we wish, an additional *sou* will procure us a table-napkin. We eat, leisurely or fast, but we need be in no hurry, and may take time to notice the many respectable occupants of other tables, even single women, who look like governesses or ladies out shopping for the day, feeding as comfortably and decorously as ourselves. Our repast ended, we lay our *carte* on the counter; it is added up in the twinkling of an eye by the clerk, usually a woman too, who sits there; we pay, and the thing is done. No fees to the waitresses—M. Duval reckons all that in their salaries. Their civility is genuine, and quite independent of a possible *sou*.

"If necessary, even a *gourmand* can dine at the Bouillons Duval. One may see figuring on the *carte* St. Julien at three francs, and Champagne at four francs fifty centimes the bottle. But these are beyond the usual requirements of M. Duval's customers.

"A word about the great man himself. He was born in 1811, at Montlhéry. At twenty he was a poor butcher-boy in Paris; at thirty he found himself, by his own industry, on the high road to fortune. He has had many failures, many disappointments, but has overcome them all. M. Duval is a man of middle stature, brown-complexioned, red-bearded, with brown hair. He speaks much, and with a natural and proud satisfaction, of all he has done and all he means to do. Nothing is too fine for him—nothing too great. 'Still, take care of the money,' whispers gently Madame Duval.

"Ordinarily the husband follows the advice of the wife, as all good husbands should do; but in this case he has not done it. In the lavishly splendid procession of the *Bœuf Gras* M. Duval has listened to nobody, unless it be to his classically-educated son, in describing to him the costumes of Greece and Rome."

Very grand the costumes were, and accurate likewise. And if under Minerva's helmet, or the flowery garland of May (who had hard work, poor soul, to quiet a hungry, thinly-clad, rather obstreperous baby), were faces not absolutely classical, which looked worn, sallow, and pinched in the sharp morning air, why, what could you expect? I only hope M. Duval gave each of his gods and goddesses a real good mortal dinner at one of his *bouillons*.

Besides these live personages, the mechanical appliances of the show were very good. I still recall with a childish satisfaction the big, calm (artificial) sphinx, sitting with her paws stretched out, and her eyes gazing right forward, as is the custom of sphinxes; the huge stuffed elephant, a little shaky on the legs, but majestic still; and, above all, the gigantic *bœuf*, made of colored bladders, that floated airily over the last *char*, attached only by a slender string. This string was cut just in front of the balcony of the Tuileries, when the extraordinary animal soared at once skyward, balloon fashion, to the ecstasy—the newspapers record—of the young Prince Imperial, and causing even the grim Emperor himself to break into a smile.

Whenever during the three days we met the procession, an eager crowd always followed, flattening itself against railings, filling street-doorways, and raising itself in tier after tier of heads upon the steps of churches, just as our crowds do, only with twice as much merriment and good-humor. And when, though tracking it out of Paris proper to the suburban district of Les Ternes, we still felt its results in having to sit for twenty minutes in the last of a row of six omnibuses all *complet*, but each waiting patiently the hour of starting, we could not help noticing its exceeding cheerfulness. All the passengers chattered away together in the shrillest and most joyous French, but nobody complained of the long delay—nobody scolded the conductor. I do not say the French are a better race than we, but they are certainly better-tempered, especially when out for a holiday.

Mardi-Gras, the last day of the festival, brought a sight which I shall not soon forget. It was a lovely spring evening, and down the Champs Elysées the people swarmed like bees in the sunshine, all classes and ranks together. Some drove down the centre way in handsome carriages, mostly filled with children, whose happy faces peered brightly over the white fur or bearskin rugs which enwrapped them. Others, well-dressed and respectable folk, sat in groups on the chairs and benches, as if it were summer-time; while the "lower orders," as we call them, formed one smooth settled line along the edge of the *pavé*, behind which was another line continually in motion, until at the Place de la Concorde it coagulated into one compact mass.

There the people stood, the setting sun shining on their merry faces, on the very spot where, scarcely a generation ago, their fathers and mothers had seen the "son of St. Louis" remorselessly executed; whence afterward his queen and widow gave that last pathetic glance toward the Tuileries Gardens, and died silently, a queen to the end. Sad and strange! infinitely sad and strange! Almost incredible, one would think, watching the Paris of to-day. But as one traverses that wonderful modern city, yearly changing so fast—new streets, avenues, and faubourgs rising, until historical Paris is almost entirely obliterated—("It is not desirable for us to have a history," said a Parisian one day to me)—one can not help wondering what will be the story of the future—what new events, what possible tragedies may still be enacted there.

But the only tragedy to-day was that of the *Bœuf Gras*, which, after his three days' triumph, was now borne relentlessly to the Palais de l'Industrie. All that crowd was waiting to see him enter there, never to emerge again except as beef. Yet he had had his day. Portraits of him were circulating about the streets, one of which— a splendid broadside—we bought. It contains, besides a gorgeous engraving of the procession, two poems, one of which has a curious thread of pathos running through its buffoonery. Here it is, done into English from its Nivernais *patois:*

"Le Dernier Voyage de Gulliver.

"Ha! ha! the fever of success
   Burns in my veins. So fat—so fair!
Of all the oxen of Nièvre
   I am the biggest and most rare;
All envy me, the beast of price,
And from my flank will have a slice;
Alas! to be too beautiful
Is dangerous both to man—and bull!

When in my village home I dwelt,
   How happy was I all day long!
Now in a gilded car I ride,
   The glory of the Paris throng.
The Carnival—the Carnival,
I am the centre of it all!
But, ah! to be so much caressed
Is good for neither man nor beast.

Once in my quiet country meads
   I cropped the cool delicious grass:
Beside my sweet companion cow
   How cheerful, how content I was!
Now parted from my better half,
I moan and pine like any calf;
And torn from her, green fields, fresh air,
I weep my lot in being too fair!

Adieu, fat pastures that I loved!
   Adieu, my innocent pleasures all!
My last, last journey now I take
   To grace the Paris Carnival.
What fate is mine! I ride in state,
Descend, am killed, and cooked, and ate.
Alas! to be too beautiful
Is death alike to man—and bull!"

There is a second poem, "*Causerie d'un Bœuf masqué*," but it is written in such queer *patois*, and so full of puns and references to the Paris slang of the day, that I should despair of making it intelligible either in French or English. But it is at least quite harmless, which is more than can be said of every thing Parisian.

Nevertheless, perfectly harmless, so far at least as we witnessed it—which was up to ten o'clock P.M.—on *Mardi-Gras*, seemed the fun of the Paris streets, carnival fun though it was. We quitted the thronged Place de la Concorde with the sun setting upon the poor *bœuf's* last hour of life, and very thankful to know the victim was only a *bœuf*; nor did we reappear again on the surface of the city till 8 P.M., when its aspect had altogether changed—

At first, rather for the worse. Every shop was shut. The bright line of the Boulevards was now one long darkness. All those cheery *boutiques* where *Madame la boutiquière* may generally be seen composedly sitting at her evening work, or chatting with her friends, were closed and silent. Here and there only, in some of the paved alleys, there was a photographer's window or a cigar-shop open, to illuminate the spot. But to various places of amusement—theatres, masqued balls, and so on—there were endless directions; guiding stars done in gas, and flaring gas inscriptions, to attract the crowd. It thickened and thickened, until it flowed down the pavement in three continuous streams, two downward and one upward, chiefly composed of the under-world, the working world of Paris; but, so far as we could judge, entirely respectable. All were strictly decorous in their dress, manners, and behavior; and as they gathered round the few illuminated windows, the light showed their faces to be no worse than most holiday faces—perhaps better; for the universal white cap and neat *capuchon* gave to the women an air of decent grace which one rarely sees under the flaunting, shabby, flower-bedecked bonnets of the corresponding class in London. Most of them, whether young or elderly, were escorted by some male friend, husband or sweetheart, upon whose arm, or both his arms, they merrily hung, to the detriment of his invariable cigar. But I can not say the Paris men are either so attractive or so respectable-looking as the Paris women.

By-and-by, the night being fine, the spaces in front of the restaurants began to fill. The crowd settled down to take its *café* as usual in the open air. Soon there was a three-deep row of crowded tables, at which sociable family groups chatted and looked about them, and sipped various beverages of apparently innocuous kind. Drink is, apparently, not the temptation of a Frenchman; not a single drunken man did we see during the whole three days. Would it be so if we had a London carnival?

Nor was there, in spite of the continually increasing crowd, any inconvenient pushing or crushing. That thoroughly French civility and courtesy, which I have so often referred to, never failed. Once only there was any thing approaching to a rush—when a party of young men and women, dressed for the Opera-ball in fancy costumes, stopped to take their *café*, visible to all outsiders, at a restaurant. But even then the result was only a scramble and a good stare, the sole expression of feeling on the part of the crowd coming from a peasant-lad, who lifted up his hands and eyes in admiration of the women, exclaiming " *C'est éblouissant !*"

But soon the throng became almost impassable, especially round the *costumiers'* shops, where, surrounded by a blaze of satin dominoes, white, black, pink, scarlet, and backed by queer masks of all sorts, sempstresses were seen diligently stitching—hard at work while all Paris was at play—upon ball-costumes. And presently one saw now and then, threading the crowd in their masques and dominoes, people who were going to " assist" at that final festivity, the grand masqued ball at the Opéra Comique—said to be the most splendid, attractive, and disgraceful recreation of the city in its holiday mood—at which, I need scarcely say, we were not present. But we caught floating fragments of it pushing through the streets, or humble imitations of it done by ragged lads squeaking in horrible cows' horns from under gigantic noses; while older and less innocent young fools, dressed up in women's clothes, shrieking in shrill treble, and waving broken parasols about their heads, occasionally darted through the crowd, which made way for them, and greeted them with shouts of appreciative laughter. We thought it was time to go home—and went.

At eight o'clock next morning, entering, as was my wont, the nearest church, I met crowds—actual crowds, of both men and women hurrying to its doors. All sorts of people they were—the working-class, the shop-keeping class—the same class exactly which had filled the streets up to ten o'clock on the night before. Now, at that early hour in the morning, they were beginning their day by going to *basse messe*, or confession, or whatever it was—I never have understood the ins and outs of Roman Catholic services, which to us seem so childish and involved. But of one thing I am certain—the people *pray*. And it was a curious and startling contrast to all the mirth and revelry of the past three days, to see them turn out thus, on a gloomy, damp morning, to commence with earnest worship—at least their countenances implied earnestness—the first day of *Carême;* what we call Ash-Wednesday.

"*Les Anglais n'aiment pas s'amuser.*" No. I am afraid we do not. Races, like individuals, have their special characteristics, which it is useless to fight against, and almost useless to try to alter. Best to leave them as they are, when they are mere "peculiarities," not degenerating into actual sins. Therefore I am not going to add one word of moralizing—not, certainly, of condemnation—either of ourselves or our neighbors. Only, that if there are better things, there certainly may be worse, than this sight which I have here recorded of a City at Play.

CHAPTER IV.

A PARIS SUNDAY.

Not at all the kind of Sunday that Continental travelers often spend—acting on the principle of doing at Rome as the Romans do—ignoring their decent, British, sabbatical ways, and joining, nothing loth, in foreign fashions; nay, visiting, since there is nobody there to see, exhibitions, concerts, promenades, and even Sunday-evening theatres. We did nothing of this, and yet I fear our Sunday was not exactly a rest-day; in fact, it was spent in a sort of religious dissipation. From eight A. M. to five P.M. we were constantly at church, or, more correctly speaking, at churches.

We wanted to see how the more seriously-minded half of Paris comports itself on a Sunday, or whether it has any strong feeling about the day at all; which, at first, one feels inclined to doubt, for both French Catholics and French Protestants, however devout, do not regard the Sabbath in the strict Mosaic light which many of us do, and are far more latitudinarian—or liberal—which you will—in its observance. Above all, we wished thoroughly to see, and fairly to judge, those fine Roman Catholic services which our English Ritualistic churches labor so freely to imitate, believing—as I think they do believe in all sincerity—that if we could only revive dead outside forms, the sleeping spirit of religious faith would soon be reanimated into earnest life. Visionary hope! which reminds one somewhat of those pathetic child funerals—I think, in South America—where it is the custom to dress the little corpse in its best attire, put a gilt crown over the sunken forehead, garlands and playthings in the stiffened fingers, and so carry it in procession through the streets, as if alive; yet it is but a corpse, after all. Alas! something more than gorgeous vestments, flower-decked altars, and picturesque churches is needed to rouse in any dead soul the true spirit of religious belief—the life " hid with Christ in God."

I do not say we found this, but we tried to seek for it both in Catholic and Protestant worship, and I dare not say we could not find it, or that it was not there. Of the four services we attended, differing as they did, there was yet in each something with which any devout Christian might honestly sympathize, if he went in the spirit of sympathy and not of opposition. I say this deliberately and fearlessly, because it seems to me that even good Christians do not feel half strongly enough that pure religious faith delights less in negatives than affirmatives; in agreeing with our brothers in as many points as we can, and passing over the rest, as matters solely between him and his God, instead of hunting out with " flaw-seeking eyes like needle-points" the various subjects upon which we so differ from him, and resolutely and fiercely ignoring those upon which we might possibly agree.

Now, without wishing to offend a large body of most sincerely pious people, I must own that I have no horror whatsoever of the Pope, and that " the beast" and the " woman in scarlet" never come into my head, even in the most obnoxious of Catholic churches. I can look on all their beautiful "idolatries"—as Exeter Hall would say—as calmly as a man looks on a ballroom *belle* or a siren of the stage, recognizing her various claims to admiration, but without the slightest intention or desire to marry her. Nevertheless, speaking of idolatries, I think we somewhat misjudge our Catholic brethren on this head; we take for granted, not what they *say* they believe, but what we *think* they believe, and judge them less by their real creed than our own presumed interpretation of it. As a rule, intelligent, rational Catholics always protest that they do not "worship" their images, but merely hold them in reverence as helps to devotion —which, by the way, considering how puerile and almost ludicrous most of them are, is one of the oddest and most contradictory facts in the Catholic religion.

One of the few French churches in which one's taste —one's artistic taste, I mean—is not continually offended, is the ancient church of St. Roch, in the Rue St. Honoré. To pass out of the noisy, busy street—busy even at early morning, and on a Sunday morning—into its quiet, sombre shadow, gives a sense of indescribable peace. Then there is such a strange, weird light shed— I know not how, probably by concealed yellow glass— upon its high altar; its painted windows are all so wondrously beautiful, and the various religious pictures and sculptures with which it is adorned are of sufficiently high art to be, at all events, no actual hinderance to the feelings which they were meant to excite. There are, for instance, in a chapel at the eastern end, two groups, somewhat above life size, of the Crucifixion and the Entombment, startlingly vivid in their conception, and very fine in their execution—especially the first one. The Savior lies prone—extended on the as yet unlifted cross, to which two soldiers are in the act of nailing, one a hand, the other a foot. Both pause, as if appealing to the centurion standing by—"Must we do this thing?"— but the Christ speaks not at all. Infinite submission is written on His face. And I think even a stanch Protestant—knowing how hard is this lesson, which we must all learn after him—might stand and gaze at the figure, lying so still and white in the sacred silence of the early morning, and accept from it a mute sermon, as good as many an anti-papal thunderbolt fulminated from some pulpits I could name.

St. Roch has numerous small chapels—nooks where any weary soul may go in and pray, almost unobserved. These, on that Sunday morning, were sprinkled with many of these solitary, motionless figures, chiefly women, which, to me, are the most touching sight in Roman Catholic churches. They come for no external form of worship, putting on their best go-to-meeting bonnet, joining with or criticising their neighbor in a regular service; they just creep in quietly, kneel down and pray on their own account, and for some strong personal need. I can never pass one of them—so quiet, so absorbed—without wondering what blessing is to be implored—what sorrow to be averted—all the countless secrets that every human soul must have; and, however blind I may deem the prayer, I dare not—I would not if I dared—look with aught but reverence upon my brother or sister "that prayeth."

Besides these individual worshipers, I found at St.

Roch, early as it was, not much past eight A.M., a considerable congregation—in fact, two distinct congregations, assembled before the two principal altars, at each of which was going on the *basse messe*, which every priest is bound to celebrate once a day. Those who attended it were chiefly the better order of working people, though there were some very poor—poorer than any of the folk who venture into our churches on Sunday; but here they are not afraid. There was also a large sprinkling of Sisters of Charity, paying their religious devotions before entering on their day's work of practical service—how hard and how nobly done, probably none could judge except a Sister of Charity. I never can look without respect upon these rough black gowns, those frightful white poked caps or bonnets, which often hide such sweet, saintly, and even beautiful faces.

One of them, which happened to be close beside me, will rest on my memory for years. She was quite a girl, certainly not five-and-twenty, with features correct as a piece of statuary. I never saw a lovelier outline of mouth, cheek, and chin, melting rosily down into a throat that was absolutely perfect in color and form. And the expression—so still, so absorbed, as she knelt utterly unconscious of my gaze, counting her beads with fingers that, in spite of the injury of hard work, were still finely shaped; thorough "aristocratic" hands—Raffaelle would have made her into a Madonna at once! One could not help thinking, Who was she? what had been her history? Could any great anguish have awakened this religious ecstasy which had led her to resolve to be nobody's wife, nobody's mother, but to spend her life in the incessant, often repulsive labors of a Sister of Charity? Would the impulse last? Would no natural human regrets ever arise, causing her to reflect of her vow? I left her kneeling there, utterly engrossed in her rapt devotion, and unconscious that she had been the object of such deep admiration, such earnest speculations. She goes down among the list of living pictures which a student of humanity is so often meeting, and which, to my mind, are as interesting as any fine-art galleries in the world.

This *basse messe* always seems to me the most expressionless and empty of all religious services—a mere mumbling and muttering, without audible words to dignify and make it comprehensible; while, on the other hand, it has none of the outside shows, the music especially, which appeal to the heart without need of words. But the congregation seemed quite satisfied, and knelt in their places with reverent air, sincerely convinced that they were serving God in their own way. As doubtless they were, but it was not my way; so I soon quietly departed.

In passing one of the old men who sit at the doors offering to outgoers the funny little brush of holy water, he, no doubt recognizing a daily visitor to the church, held it out to me, but I shook my head; at which, good soul, he took no offense, but meekly drew back his brush, and answered, with civil *empressement*, some questions about high mass, which was to be celebrated that morning. Nay, thinking he had not made it clear enough, the poor old fellow almost jumped out of his box to call after me, "*Madame! Madame! Onze heures, à onze heures précis. La grande messe avec la musique!*" As much as to say, " Don't miss it upon any account, and you will see what will make you a good Catholic to the end of your days."

No, my friend, it didn't, and moreover I doubt if any thing ever would. Never could I resign my own plain common sense, reason, or faith, to be led blindfold by any man alive, not to speak of that conglomeration of men which call themselves " Holy Mother Church." Far better live orphaned forever, or recognize only the one Father—God.

Nevertheless, I will confess I was deeply interested— strongly affected—by seeing for the first time that splendid show—before which our best Ritualistic imitations are tawdry shams—the regular Sunday high mass in a fine Roman Catholic church. This being the first Sunday in Lent, the adornments of the church itself were much less than usual; indeed, if I recollect right, the altar was not decked out at all, and there was a general impression of blackness—black draperies, chairs, and so on, spreading a certain sombreness of effect. But the music—my poor old janitor might well urge it upon me, for it was divine.

When we entered they were singing the " Kyrie Eleison" out of one of Mozart's most noted masses. Wave upon wave it came, " Eleison! Eleison! Kyrie Eleison! Christe Eleison!" sometimes in a boy's voice, clear, angelic—I am sure the angels must sing like little boys— sometimes in the deep roll of some voices which they have at this church of St. Roch, two or three of the grandest, solidest basses I ever heard. They used quite to overwhelm me with their majestic pathos, until, one chance morning service, I happened to sit near the owners of them, three very ugly and not too cleanly little Frenchmen, who looked exactly like what I believe they were, respectable "*épiciers.*" Of course, these are the "stage effects" common to most forms of worship. The Roman Catholic has them to a greater extent than many.

Nevertheless, high mass possesses, in common with its opposite pole, the Quaker service, one great merit — it leaves one very much to one's self. Many a time, when in English or Scotch churches, I have longed to go into a Friends' Meeting-house, and sit there, dead silent, with every one else mercifully silent likewise, for the whole two hours. Instead, how often is one goaded into thinking that any kind of dumb worship — even the Indian faquir, who stands all day on his head in the sun — would be preferable to having to sit and listen to a man who goes talking on about things which he neither comprehends himself nor makes you comprehend; or, if you do, you wholly differ from him, yet can not rise and protest, telling him that his whole argument is based on premises taken for granted, but as yet entirely unproved; or that six verses out of the Bible would be more acceptable than all his discourse.

But silence, or very fine music, are devotional expressions in which all worshipers can meet upon equal footing, because, throughout, each man preaches to himself his own sermon. I believe it was no sacrilegious worship to sit an hour in St. Roch's, without either prayer-book or hymn-book, and drink in that glorious music — music with scarcely intelligible words — which carried one away in thought to the choir of saints and angels, and all the innumerable company of the happy dead, to which we trust we shall one day go. And, though not quite agreeing with that good man, who, at the close of a funeral sermon, once assured his hearers that their life in heaven would be singing hallelujahs forever and ever (which—I remember thinking—some of his congregation would not like at all)—still, as all real music-lovers feel, there is something in a body of harmonious sound more utterly spiritual, more approximating to what we ascribe to the nature of spirit, than any thing else in this world. All other sensuous delights can be touched, tasted, handled, or at least beheld; this one is wholly intangible and invisible, nothing in itself, and apparently evoked from nothing; when it ceases, it ceases as completely as if it never had been—at least to all our human senses. Yet while it lasted it was a real thing—an ecstatic sensation, as perfect as any sensation we know—and may be revived at will into the same vivid existence.

I once heard it said by a musician who now comprehends it all, that his nearest conception of pure "spirit" was the sound of one of Handel's choruses; and I never hear fine music, finely executed, such as this mass of Mozart's in St. Roch, without feeling the same.

There was a pause in the service, first when the tall *huissier* went round preceding an unctuous-looking priest, who, in the usual whining voice, presented his bag "*pour l'entretien de l'église*," or briefly "*pour l'église*." Again, when two sweet-faced altar-boys—either of whom might have sat for a portrait of Chaucer's young saint, who, when some Jews decapitated him, the pretty head kept singing "Ave Maria" by itself all day and all night long—went down the aisle, and came back in procession, accompanied by two other boys carrying gigantic and very tottering lighted candles, preceding a basket of bread. At least, not exactly bread, but a sort of *brioche*, which they afterward distributed to the congregation. What was the meaning of it, or whether it was consecrated or not, I have not the least idea, but I thought in no case could it do me any harm, so I accepted and ate it. It tasted much like all other *brioches*—which seems a favorite cake in Paris—and I do not find it has made me one whit more of a Catholic than heretofore.

Then the choir music began again; the midday sun came pouring in floods through the painted windows, and shone in a stream of glory on the high altar of the rock—from which the name of the church comes, though through what legend I do not know. Very little did we ever make out, or cared to make out of their churches and services; they were just a dream of enjoyment, and, I must say, enjoyment of the keenest and most harmless kind. When the concluding strain died away, and high mass was over, we rose and departed, feeling not the slightest desire to hear it every Sunday, or to exchange for it, or any imitation of it, our own pure, simple, earnest Church Service. Nevertheless, we recognized fully that in the wonderful beauty and perfectness of this service was a something which, appealing to imaginative minds, who bring with them half they behold, might prove most soothing, elevating, and consoling, even so far as to account partially for what ever seemed to me the greatest mystery imaginable—how any rational being of mature age could ever be converted to Roman Catholicism.

As quickly as possible—one service ending and the other beginning at nearly the same hour—we drove to a very different place of worship, the French Protestant Church in the Rue de Provence. And here we made, ignorantly, the same mistake that one is prone to make in Scotland between the Established "church" and the English "chapel;" our *cocher* persisted in taking us to an "*église*"—Catholic, of course—so that it was with great difficulty we arrived at the "*chapelle*" at all. One could not help smiling at these verbal distinctions, which are yet so natural, nay, right. Probably Ireland is the only country in the world where, by a curious, and, I think, most unjust anomaly, the religious establishment of the minority enjoys the title and privileges of a "Church."

The *chapelle* in the Rue de Provence is not the original French Protestant Church, but a branch of it, which holds much the same relation to it that the Free or United Presbyterian churches do to the Established Church of Scotland. I believe the differences are merely on points of Church government. But there is a far wider breach now taking place—the secession headed by M. Coquerel the younger, which has caused as many heart-burnings and painful divisions of families against themselves as did ever the disruption in Scotland, raising a spirit of religious animosity that in so small a community must be painful in the extreme. Alas! when will people—good people—learn that the "sword" which Christ himself declared He came to send upon earth must be only the sword of the Spirit; pure, bright, and clean; strong and sharp, "to the dividing of joints and marrow?"

That is, as regards a man's own conscience, but never to be turned against the conscience of his brothers; never to be used in any human quarrel, never to be dulled by any fleshly taint of selfish vanity or personal wrong.

Nothing could be a greater contrast than the French Catholic church we had just left, and the French Protestant one we now entered, where we found the service had just begun. It was plain even to bareness: there was apparently a scrupulous avoidance of every charm of color and form. The building seemed all in straight lines, windows included; a mere room, simple as any Dissenting meeting-house, or one of those erections of the last generation, which one finds planted, oddly enough, in some of the most picturesque points of Scotch braes and hill-sides, as if Nature loved to worship God in beauty, and man in ugliness. But no; I can not say this church was absolutely ugly, only that it was simple even to severity.

It had neither altar nor pulpit, but the same sort of rostrum which one sees in Scotch Presbyterian churches, and on it stood the pastor, a mild, benevolent-looking man, in his ordinary dress, not unlike a Scotch Free Church minister. I noticed no precentor, but there must have been one to lead the singing, which was going on at the time, the congregation *sitting* to sing, as they do in Scotland. And oh! the beauty of that hymn! What it was I know not; but just such a one might have up-risen in the night-time from Waldensian valleys, or some of those lovely nooks of Southern France where the Huguenots had their main stronghold—where they clung desperately to their faith, fought for it, died for it, with a tenacity of purpose that only the Scotch Covenanters have ever surpassed:

> "We English have a scornful insular way
> Of calling the French light."

So says Mrs. Browning in "Aurora Leigh," and proceeds to deny the "lightness"—in which I once thought she was mistaken. I do not now. No one could look round that congregation, with its faces of men and women—noble, simple, lofty; quite peculiarly so, I thought—without feeling that, Frenchmen and Frenchwomen though they were, "light" was the very last epithet which could be fairly applied to them. We are prone to judge France solely by Paris, which is about as just as if we were to judge England—that is to say, the whole of the British Islands—by London. Whether we recognize it or not, there is, in the various races which make up the aggregate French people, an element of strength, firmness, sincerity, faithfulness, as grand as any thing in our own nation. Probably it lurks deepest, and comes out clearest amid the old Huguenot blood, and in those relics of the *ancienne noblesse* and the cultivated middle class of provincial *propriétaires* which have survived the terrible winnowing-flail of the Revolution—or, say rather, the Revolutions. But of this I can not judge—no foreigner could; only I am certain it is there; and never was I more certain than in watching that congregation in the Rue de Provence.

They were somewhat different from a Catholic congregation; there was little of that *abandon* of religious fervor that one sees at a Catholic church; they were less absorbed, more critical, but still grave, decorous, correct, receptive—like an English or Scotch, but more especially a Scotch congregation. And very like a Scotch sermon translated into French, but retaining its exact forms of Calvinistic phrase, and its tone of address to "*mes chers frères*," was the discourse into which, after a short prayer and a still shorter—perhaps too short—reading of Holy Scripture, the good pastor plunged.

Of that sermon what can I say? There was nothing remarkably original in it; but the delivery was simple, dignified, sincere; and though it was extempore, the matter seemed well considered, and the language, so far as one can judge in the rapid utterance of a foreign tongue, perspicuous, elegant, and good. But I think we would have liked a little shorter sermon, and a little longer reading of *le St. Evangile*, which he did read very beautifully, in his musical, solemn, tender French—qualities which at first seem impossible to that lively language, but which, when one is familiarized with it, its childlike grace and simplicity of phrase, especially in the New Testament, has a devotional charm quite peculiar, and never to be forgotten.

It was the same with the hymns. They were neither English nor Scotch psalm-tunes, nor German chorales, and, of course, they were utterly removed from any thing in the Roman Catholic service; but they had a beauty of their own, delicious even immediately after Mozart's Grand Mass—the last hymn especially, which was sung as the people were departing; for it was a Communion Sunday, and a proportion, though not a great one, went out, the rest keeping their seats, just as in a Presbyterian church, and singing, sweetly and solemnly, a long-drawn-out and infinitely pathetic sacramental hymn, the music of which rings in my heart at this minute.

No doubt the Protestant Church of France has its weak points—what Church has not?—and probably the weakest of them are its dawning divisions, and the fierce rancor they excite, of bigotry on the one side, and fierce, youthful revolt against the bondage of compelled faith on the other. But we thought we could better understand historic France, and look forward more hopefully to the future of modern France, after having worshiped with that little congregation in the Rue de Provence.

We came out into the bleak sunshine—oh, how bitter-bleak Paris sunshine can be!—and took an hour or two's wandering through the bright streets, where the people were gradually thickening. The city had put off its devotional, and put on its holiday face for the rest of the day. It evidently agreed with the birds, who, as some good Scotchman once rather regretfully observed, "went on singing just as if it wasn't Sunday." These good French folks—chiefly of the *bourgeoisie*—their wives and daughters, loitered about, looking in at all the shop-windows that were open, which included nearly every one in the Rue de Rivoli; and I own I should like to have gone with a *gendarme* down the whole length of the street and closed them all, saying, "Rest, perturbed spirits; rest, if you can do no more." Then they hung in clusters round the doors of country-bound omnibuses in the square of the Palais Royal, or went in little bands to the noble galleries of the Louvre, with all its stores of centuried learning, that he who runs may read—a source of Sabbath instruction and amusement which I, for one, should be very sorry to deny them. For the rest, they went about their several ways, and comported themselves much as Parisian Sunday-afternoon promenaders usually do. They harmed us not, and no comments shall be made upon them: we English have too many glass houses of our own to afford to throw stones.

It was more by chance than design that we fell in for our next service, perhaps the most curious of all. Entering a church to rest—and, oh, the rest to tired soul and body that those dim, cool, silent churches are sometimes!—we found it was St. Germain l'Auxerrois, notable in history as being the one from whose tower had sounded the warning bell, the signal for the massacre of St. Bartholomew. The slaughter began there, and in the Palace of the Louvre just opposite, continuing all throughout Paris, till by morning the Seine—this slow, quiet, muddy Seine, which we had stood calmly watching—ran red with blood.

A terrible story—and it all happened here—just here. No wonder at a certain firmness, nay, hardness, in those grave Protestant faces worshiping in the Rue de Provence. One could imagine what their ancestors and ancestresses' faces must have been; one can understand the maddened despair, capable of any courage, any fury, of these husbandless wives and childless mothers, and how they would develop into those stern, rigid Puritan women, who have left their remembrances stamped vividly even upon the present generation. Solemn, strange, and yet grand beyond the grandeur of most human existences would be a life of which the key-note was—as I once heard a soft, quiet old voice say, returning to long-past days—"When my father was *murdered*."

This is the difference between modern France and England. Our tragedies, political and religious, mostly lie far back in the past, dim as old romance; theirs are scarce a generation removed from the daily present. The veil between is so thin that they feel the past might at any time be repeated in the present.

St. Germain l'Auxerrois is a very beautiful church, brighter and *younger* looking, so to speak, than St. Roch, without having the unpleasant modernness and pseudo-classicality of the Madeleine. The painted glass is fine, and the high altar has less than the average of foolish fripperiness about it. There is the usual broad, circumferent walk, interspersed with the usual number of quaint little chapels; nooks where some may pray, and all may rest and meditate, not without advantage. In several of these was going on a sort of Sunday-school—different classes of little boys and girls standing, with grave little faces, book in hand, to be catechised by some priest, generally a young man, who seemed to take much pains with them, and to whom they were very attentive.

Suddenly, high up in the tower outside began to sound —not the awful tocsin of St. Bartholomew, and yet it might have been the self-same bell—a common church bell, with its steady monotone. I asked my neighbor, a decent-looking *bonne*, in charge of a young lady, who knelt absorbed before an altar of the Virgin, what it was ringing for. "*Les Vêpres*," said she, briefly and severely. Then this was the immemorial "vesper-bell," though most unpoetically ringing at three in the afternoon.

However, we thought we would remain and see what there was to be seen.

Gradually there collected in front of the high altar a moderate congregation, chiefly composed of women; and, when the bell ceased, there came filing in a line of priests richly vestmented, and another line of little boys, whose dress, I think, was of scarlet and white, but I do not clearly remember. They and the priests began the service with the ever-beautiful harmony of boys' and men's voices singing alternately or together, which the Catholic Church so well knows how to use.

Vespers is, I conclude, a litany rather than a mass. Many of the congregation joined in it out of their prayer-book, and it seemed to be in French, not Latin. It was less fine than the service at St. Roch, and yet a beautiful service in its way, or would have been but for the ludicrous effect produced by two young priests, who kept marching slowly up and down, reading their breviaries, stopping at every third turn to seat themselves solemnly on two high stools, over and outside which they carefully disposed their robes, said a prayer or two, then got up again and renewed their walk. What it all meant I have not the slightest idea, but the result was comical to a degree, especially the feminine care in the arrangement of the violet velvet.

This and the singing went on for about an hour; then the priests marched in single file out of the chancel, and as they passed we noticed them sharply.

I must confess, these magnificent robes are not surmounted by the noblest faces in the world. It is curious, if true—and I do think it is true—that certain phases of religious belief always result in certain types of face, or, more correctly, it is the personal idiosyncrasy as shown by the face which causes a certain line of religious thinking. You will hardly ever find combined a narrow creed and a broad forehead; a fat, sensuous jowl and an ascetic faith. The Catholic priesthood do not, as a body, look like men of intellect or refinement. Here and there I have seen some fine, benevolent heads — quite apostlelike—but, in the main, they are coarse and common, evidently taken from the lower classes, and educated only to a certain point—the point beyond which a human being ceases to be a mere machine, thinks spontaneous thoughts, and indulges in original acts, which might be rather inconvenient in a system of such total self-repression as the Catholic Church. These men, principally old men, had all the air of devoutness; but it was a dull, solid, not to say stupid air, implying superstition rather than faith, and the lazy following of others' opinions rather than that wide-eyed search after truth for truth's own sake, which is the only thing which makes a religious man a true priest.

After they had passed and settled themselves in a long row opposite the pulpit, the congregation also turned their chairs round so as to face the same way; more hearers gathered, until inside and outside of their middle inclosure there was hardly standing-room. We looked intently toward the pulpit, where suddenly appeared a man in a monk's dress. We had come in for one of those Lenten sermons with which the Catholic Church, wisely distinguishing the vast difference between an ordinary priest and a really good preacher, is careful to provide her devotees during the fast. That this was a very popular *prédicateur* the eagerness of the crowded congregation plainly showed. Who he was we knew not, nor does it matter; but he was a man of about fifty years of age, with a keen, mobile face, rather roughly cut—a little "underbred," one might have said, had one met him in ordinary life; but of his exceeding ability there could be no doubt.

He waited till the mass of the people had settled and hushed duly into attention; then he rose, and with a few preliminary bowings and crossings, began his sermon in a low, measured voice, gradually advancing into distinctness, power, and passion, till it rung through the whole church, where, as the phrase is, "you might have heard a pin fall."

Alas! it is only too few sermons that one *can* remember, but I shall long remember this, Catholic though it was. There was not a sentence in it to which a good Protestant might not have listened with advantage. Its subject was "*La Parole de Dieu*," "sharper than a two-edged sword," and so on—I can not call to mind the exact text; indeed, I rather think it began without any text, but this was the theme of it: *la Parole de Dieu*, as heard by man throughout life, whether consciously or not; heard in nature, in human affections, in religious devotions, in all the events and crises of existence. In short, the Voice of God to man, forever calling, calling.

The preacher began by a vivid picture of the earliest dawn of life—the child in the cradle, encircled by household love, *la Parole de Dieu* only speaking to it through the lips of parents. He described with a tender vividness, that was strange to hear from him—poor celibate! —the happiness of father and mother bending over their first-born, and all the after-scenes of family bliss; then traced the boy through youth and manhood, *la Parole de Dieu* still speaking to him under all manner of forms, and in every conceivable circumstance, forcing him at last to hear; because God is his Father, and the Father will not let go His child.

"But," continued the preacher, suddenly changing into the personal, and bursting into something very like eloquence—French eloquence, it must be remembered—with abundance of gesture, with an impetuosity of delivery that in an English pulpit would be called theatrical—and yet it never passed the verge where the dramatic becomes the mere theatrical—it never degenerated into mere acting—"but"—you say—"how am I to know that God is my Father? How can His infinite greatness care for my infinite littleness? I am an atom, less than an atom in the sight of my Creator, and the Creator of the universe. When I look abroad on Nature—" (and here he burst into gorgeous descriptions of the wonders in the heavens and earth, and under the earth). "How can we look at these, and yet know that the Maker of them all is our Father?"

"Know it? I do *not* know it. I know nothing, and attempt to know nothing. But I feel it *here*"—and he touched his breast, nay, struck it with a violence plainly audible, which cynics would certainly have called claptrap; yet I can not think it was so—not entirely. I can not believe but that there was some reality in the passionate pathos of the man's voice, as he kept repeating over and over again those words which, if we once doubt, all life becomes a dead, hopeless blank—"*Dieu est mon Père. Il m'aime, je crois qu'il m'aime.* And why? Because I feel it here. I feel that I love Him, and I could not love Him unless He had loved me first. *Il est mon Père—mon Père.*"

"And, once sure of that," he went on, "I am sure of every thing. He will give me every thing, because He is my Father. You count me unhappy? I am the happiest man alive! I am forever in the sight and presence of my Father. You think me without guidance? He leads me continually by His hand. *Il m'aime, il m'aime toujours. Dieu est mon Père.*"

These four words were the burden of the sermon. It entered upon no doctrinal questions; scarcely even laid down any moral laws; it carried the hearers quite out of the region of controversial theology into that high mountain-air of Truth—the Truth of truths—which is Love. From that clear height, if we could ever attain to it, many diverse creeds might look almost identical. But whatsoever one might doubt—whatsoever one might differ upon, the man had struck a chord which must vibrate in every heart; for the Fatherhood of God once recognized, in the individual as well as the universal sense, solves all perplexities, and makes the riddle of life clear and plain. It was good to hear it thus preached, even from a Roman Catholic pulpit.

Thus ended—and it was a peaceful, harmonious ending—our strange, contradictory, yet, looked upon in its deepest sense, this our most solemn Paris Sunday. We never heard who the preacher was; indeed, we never inquired: good and true words being said, it matters little who says them. But these words of his made us come out of church—that terrible bloodstained church of St. Germain l'Auxerrois—with a wonderfully calm and happy feeling, sure that, after all, *la Parole de Dieu,* "sharper than a two-edged sword," is the sharpest and strongest thing in all this world. Also, that if God is our Father indeed (and if not that, He is nothing, does not exist for us as God at all), He will eventually make every thing clear and right, reconciling all things to Himself—all things and all men. So, over the whirl and noise of this twilight Paris—this marvelous, beautiful, dreadful city, which seems to chatter about Him so much, and to understand and believe in Him so little—there seemed to sound, wild as Jonah's voice in Nineveh, and sweet as another and diviner voice in the streets of Jerusalem, the preacher's cry, "*Dieu est mon Père.*"

CHAPTER V.

AN OLD FRENCH TOWN.

I was growing nearly wild with the whirl of Paris. To people unused to cities, and taking no natural delight in them, the noise and confusion of any large town soon produces a feeling which I can only compare to that of a Sioux Indian or a Carribee islander caught and caged in civilization. First there comes weariness, then irritation, then a frantic desire to run away " any where—any where out of the world"—that " world" which delights in streets and squares, gazing in at shop-windows and promenading in parks, with intermediate morning calls and evening reunions, where we all smile and look so sweet, knowing the whole time that—

But let me not be cynical or unjust. There are doubtless as many good people in towns as there are in the country, only, perhaps, the good would be better still if they lived in the country. They would not have their nerves torn, their tempers aggravated, and their strength exhausted in the frantic jostle of city life; they would be able to meditate as well as to work, to feel as well as to enjoy. That restless craving after excitement, the perpetual hunger for something new, which one so often sees in town-bred people, in the country dies out for lack of nutriment. There you are, perforce, thrown back upon yourself to find your own mental food—find it, or starve; which is the reason, I opine, that a certain number of natures do starve, and rush back wildly into city life, where they have not to cater for their own amusement, but can find plenty of people to feed them with all sorts of pabulum—good, bad, indifferent—if they have only the money to pay for it. No blame to these; still there are others who prefer a peaceful, self-dependent, self-contained life, where all their food is of their own earning, and to such every city becomes, after a short time, intolerable.

Paris is a degree less so than London. Its roar and confusion are not so great, its distances not so exhausting. Besides, its atmosphere is so much clearer and brighter that many people declare they are "always cheerful in Paris." Well, and it is a cheerful city; and one goes about it with a sense of real enjoyment for a while. But those hapless folk I have alluded to, who, like myself, *can not* live in cities, who after a few days suffer under a calenture of longing for green trees, soft grass, and silence—above all, silence—I can imagine lively Paris becoming to them a perfect Pandemonium.

So we made up our minds to have "a day out" for as many miles as a return journey would allow, bringing us back in time for some evening festivities which we could not miss—out neither to Versailles, Fontainebleau, St. Denis, or any of those places where Paris, and Paris visitors, are in the habit of going, but to some quiet, unknown, or unappreciated spot, where, for a few hours, we might escape into blessed country peace. And then we thought of Chartres, which, with its beautiful cathedral, had often been spoken of to us by one who well understood what beauty was, and whither we had been strongly advised to go, "because nobody ever went there," which now seemed to us the utmost desideratum.

To the extreme astonishment of the hôtel *garçon*, who could not understand how anybody, taking the *Chemin de Fer à l'Ouest*, should pass by Versailles and go on to Chartres, we extracted from him all needful information and started. It was a gray morning—not actually wet, but looking as if it would have liked to rain if it could, if the keen cold wind would let it; and we had the usual long waiting at the terminus, in that wonderful patience which all French *voyageurs* seem to possess, but which is rarely the peculiarity of the British tourist. And as dull-looking as the day were our fellow-travelers—a big, coarse farmer, with enormous hands, and a young fellow—I believe Parisian slang would give him some name answering to our word "swell," only indicating a feebler, more foppish, and generally inferior animal—though the creature was good-looking in a sort of way, too. His hair was long, his hands were long, and his finger-nails reminded one of a genteel Nebuchadnezzar: they must have been the care and the terror of his life. His dress was partial evening dress, and he looked as if he had been up all night dancing; which, it being just past the Carnival, was not improbable. His manner was languidly elegant, and he seemed to think about nothing in particular. Life was evidently a great burden to him; a "bore," in short; and, though it was little past 10 A.M., he soon took refuge in sleep. Cynical Britons would set him down contemptuously as "just a Frenchman," but I shall pass him over as an exaggeration or deterioration rather than a fair type of *la grande*

F

nation, as it calls itself, and which, in spite of our criticisms, has something greater in it than we know.

Once only did this lethargic young gentleman rouse himself sufficiently to tell us, in a faint drawl, where was the palace of Versailles—the back view of it, and a very ugly view too. Up to that point the country had been uninteresting: flat, tame, and villa-haunted, what we should call Cockneyfied; but now we got into something like rurality, and it was very refreshing to see the green fields, the hedges, and trees; bare, but still tinged with that faint reddish shade of swelling buds, which shows they are beginning to dream of spring. But there was nothing at all picturesque or beautiful to be seen, even at Versailles. The nearest approach to the picturesque was that ruined aqueduct, begun by Louis XIV., and, after three years of lavish labor, left incomplete. Its fine arches still remain visible for leagues along the hill-side, like fragments of a grand imperfect life.

We watched them, moralizing, while the train rested a moment at the little station of Maintenon, near where is the old castle which Louis XIV. gave to Veuve Scarron, and whence she took her name—that remarkable woman, who, with all her faults, was the good angel of the *Grande Monarque*, over whom she exercised a silent influence deeper than any acknowledged queenship. This, in spite of her waning beauty and advancing age—for she was fifty years old when the king married her. It is somewhat touching to read of the childless woman's devotion to "*mes enfans*" of Saint Cyr—the girls' school she founded, now turned into the well-known college for young men. We had passed the station "Saint Cyr" on the road, and thought of Madame de Maintenon and this last home, where, after her strange and brilliant career, she died at last, old and lonely, except for the "*enfans*" of her adoption. One can not help lingering over these dead and gone people, wondering how we should think of them, and feel toward them, if they could "come alive again;" whether they would seem to march with the step of gods, or be no larger than those of our own generation —now common mortals like ourselves, but whom history will elevate into heroes and heroines.

Our languid friend might be one of them—who knows? —or he might have carried in his veins the blood of that old time, before there came the grand crash of patrician and plebeian. In those days, no doubt, he would have turned up his large, well-cut nose at the common people as much as any of the rest of them—these poor mad "aristocrats," who themselves helped to light the match of the powder-magazine which destroyed them; but times were changed now. He had to sit calmly in his corner of the ordinary railway carriage, a mere passenger, and endure the intrusion of another passenger—a little, yellow-faced, white-capped old woman, carrying, in large gloved hands, an ordinary market-basket. She examined us all with her acute, black, bead-like eyes, and then settled herself in her place—next to the young dandy—with composure. She had paid her money, and had as good a right to travel first-class express as he; a fact which her self-possessed politeness indicated quite sufficiently to all comers. But we could not help smiling, thinking of the difference between the days of Louis XIV. and Madame de Maintenon and our own.

Chartres at last. We recognized it at once by the stately cathedral towering clear above the little town; not a town possessing a cathedral, but a cathedral with a small appendage of a town, which sits admiringly at its feet, and looks up to it with infinite respect—just as we do when we happen to have a great man in the family. Well, and it must be a pleasant pride to have a great man in the family, and I have always thought it would be a very pleasant thing to live in a cathedral town, and glorify one's self in it, and admire it profoundly, and love it dearly. It would be a kind of architectural hero-worship—almost as enviable in its way as to have a noble progenitor; dear as a human father should be, and yet revered as one reveres by self-election the great men of the earth.

Eagerly we descended, and emerged from the railway; but the great man had disappeared behind his humbler relations: the cathedral was blotted out by the houses of the town—gray, irregular, old-fashioned, sloping up the low hill-side from some public walk or other, and looking—oh bliss!—as if it were leagues upon leagues removed from Paris, and as if a modern villa had not been built in the place for centuries.

And entering the market-square, the Place des Epars, as our guide-book informed us, we found it occupied by a large horse-fair, carried on apparently just as it may have been carried on for centuries.

It was very different from an English fair—one could hardly say in what: still, there was a general outlandishness about every thing, which probably strikes people who have spent all their lives at home more sharply than it would those accustomed to foreign traveling. The very horses seemed tied up in a different way—and here I must protest that it was in a much crueler way—by ropes fastened round the under lips instead of the ordinary halter. I am sure if they could protest against it they would, even though their very neighing had been in French, as we fancied it sounded.

The men who attended them were like—and yet how unlike!—the same set of men which one finds at an English fair. Equally unlike—as different as Buckinghamshire plowmen from Cockneys—were they from the Parisians we had left fifty miles behind. The whole type of race had changed. The sharp city face, and small, wiry, active frame was merged into a larger limbed, honest loutishness; not the same as British loutishness, but still essentially provincial, and—dare I say it?—refreshing accordingly. It was quite comfortable to look at those tanned fellows, big and brawny, rosy, and light-haired, lounging about in their blue blouses and enormous sabots, and chattering to one another in that awful *patois*, of which we could only catch an intelligible word here and there. There were only left men enough to guard the beasts, the remainder, farmers, horse-dealers, or, as they would be called in Scotland, horse-coupers, being absent at their *déjeûner;* for it was between eleven and twelve in the forenoon.

Now nothing strikes one in different countries more curiously than the difference in feeding. Only imagine taking a British farmer at a fair, and setting him down to a midday meal of coffee, bread and butter, a few apples, or a bottle of *vin ordinaire!* Yet I declare, in all the eating-houses we passed, the Café de France, de Monarque, and several others, which surround the Place des Epars, and peering into whose wide glass windows we saw were filled with customers, I perceived no other kind of food or drink. And the consumers were stout, healthy men, large limbed and strong made. As they sat at their little marble tables, ate their enormous lumps of bread, and quaffed their innocent drink, they seemed just as merry, nay, jolly as a lot of English farmers intent upon their beef and fat bacon, their beer or brandy, ending in a condition of intoxication so common as to be considered quite inseparable from attending fairs.

In one thing, I own, my heart warms to the French peasant; he is not a drunkard. Sometimes, as we heard in Normandy, he succumbs to the influence of that wonderfully nasty compound, cider-brandy; but it is so potent, so noxious, that he drinks himself to death very soon: he does not live in that perpetual state of semi-fuddle peculiar to our beer-drinking agricultural laborer. Nor is he brought up to consider beer or spirituous liquors essential to a working-man's strength; he knows, or proves without knowing, as all simple-living, anti-wine-bibbing folks do, that alcoholic stimulant is not a necessity; that it is not a drink, but a medicine; useful in its way, as all medicines are; never to be turned into an habitual want. But this is preaching, and, cynical readers may say, without my text, since, if the French peasant could afford strong drinks, he would very likely get as drunk as any Englishman. He might; but still, at present, he does not. In all those faces which we saw about the fair, we never noticed one which was the face of a confirmed sot.

We were eager to see the cathedral, so we passed quickly through this market-square, so full of busy life, human and bestial, though the quiet horses looked almost as sensible as Christians; and there were no other animals except a few funny little calves, inclosed in pens apart, and guarded by equally funny little lads as frolicsome as themselves—lads who might have sat for the portrait of Landry, in George Sand's charming story of " La Petite Fadette;" as true, I hope, to one phase of French life as her brilliant, wonderful, horrible novels are, alas! to another. There were also a few booths erected, where two or three men were arranging for sale sundry articles—earthen-ware, iron-mongery, hosiery, linen-drapery, all of the humble and useful kind. Of fancy stores or booths of entertainment there were none; certainly the fair was one of business, not pleasure.

We quitted it, and went meandering on after the fashion so delightful in traveling, finding one's self in a perfectly strange town, where any street is quite as good as another—where one has nothing to do, and plenty of time to do it in, and every-thing one sees is sure to be amusing or interesting. At last we came into a gray, quiet street, or, rather, a congeries of streets, which might have stood just as they were since the Middle Ages.

Chartres is recorded as " one of the most ancient towns in France." Its cathedral undoubtedly dates from the beginning of the eleventh century—that is to say, contemporary with our Norman conquest—and it is not impossible to suppose that some of these houses in these substantial old streets were built by respectable burghers whose grandfathers our great-great, indefinitely great-grandfathers had killed at Cressy, Agincourt, or Poictiers. Now public buildings of antiquity are all very fine and interesting, but there is something in domestic architecture, mere houses that ordinary folk built and lived in, which is more than interesting—pathetic. One could not look at these, inhabited by the various families of a country town, year after year, and generation after generation, without thinking of the endless histories, tragic or comic, dramatic or dull, that must have been transacted within them, upon which the roughly-carved, fat-faced Gothic cherubs, which seemed the favorite doorway ornament every where, had looked so calmly, staring at all out-comers and in-goers, as they now stared at us, with their stolid stone eyes. But how difficult to realize the truth that all these people were real people, as real as ourselves, and sharing like ourselves in old Weller's comical description of himself in the character of a verb—"always a-bein', sometimes a-doin', and continiwally a-sufferin'!"

Laughing over them, but with the sadness that often lies at the root of laughter, we went on to investigate Chartres, meeting scarcely any of the inhabitants, and finding nothing very remarkable, until, seeing a priest enter a building which looked like a church, we followed him, and stood in the centre of a beautiful half-restored old chapel. But it was so full of scaffolding, hammering, noise of workmen, and clouds of falling dust, that we only stopped to watch the priest kneel down at his prayers—to him it was a consecrated place still—and hastened on, hungering for a sight of the cathedral. It was hidden, but we could occasionally catch glimpses of its two towers, not dominating over or interfering with the houses, but rising quietly above their heads (the parallel of the great man and his relations still), being always a little nearer heaven than they.

All cathedrals have their prominent characteristics: that of Chartres seemed to me to be grandeur and calm. This, in spite of its great degree of ornamentation; the front being, it is said, covered with no less than 1800 separate figures; yet it seems neither florid nor overadorned. The proportions are so immense, and yet so perfect, and the mass of Gothic figures spreads so levelly over the whole, that no special one distracts the eye; while, at the same time, if we once begin to individualize them, their beauty is endless. But the tone of color is so subdued, so soft, that they affect one like the beauty of an old woman—grander and tenderer than that of many young women, and full of the one quality in which youth fails—expression. Standing at the foot of the flight of steps, gray, old, and broken, which leads up to the entrance of Chartres Cathedral, I thought of what an artist had said the week before, in showing me the portrait of a young beauty he was at work upon—that, though youth and beauty are delightful things, still, speaking professionally, he preferred the character, the records of a lifetime's education, which time writes upon almost any middle-aged face—hieroglyphics which in all young faces must necessarily be a blank. And so it is that all deeper natures instinctively like old houses, old towns, old churches, better than any thing which is new.

At the cathedral door we came upon the very *genius*

loci in the shape of a dried-up old woman—one of those live mummies with bright black eyes, who seem peculiarly French, waiting to take from townspeople or visitors her chance of a *sou*. Above her head—curiously indicative of the sort of worshipers that visited the cathedral—was a "*défense*," forbidding entrance to all "*paniers, fardeaux, et chiens*"—something like the stern behest I once read over a Devonshire church door: "Take off your pattens!" Having none of these *impedimenta*, we walked leisurely in.

The first impression given by the interior, as well as the exterior of Chartres Cathedral, is enormous height—height rising into such dimness of shadow that it takes away the idea of any roof; one looks upward as if to the sky, and with the same sensation of peace. Amiens Cathedral has this in degree; but then Amiens still gives the feeling of newness: one is inclined to say, "How grand! and who is the architect?" But at Chartres one never thinks of the architect at all. One's soul's wings begin to tremble and stir, just as they do under the open sky, with no fragment of mortal roof, however safe and ornamental, to keep them in and restrain their liberty, even under the most beautiful bonds. I can not clearly describe the feeling; but those to whom the very breath of religious life is freedom—perfect freedom—will understand it, and what it symbolizes.

The cathedral was quite empty—that is, it seemed so at first; very silent, very dim, as if its huge aisles were always in shadow, and its rose-windows caught their colors from something far beyond common earthly sunshine; for there was none outside — the day had remained solemnly gray. But oh, the peace of the place! the heavenly quiet—the majestic calm! Entering its doors felt like the last benediction of the Catholic Church, the *vade in pacem*, dismissing a tired soul out of all the storms of life into the divine tranquillity of death.

At first we saw no sign of service going on, or of accidental worshipers, till, turning to the left, we came upon a shrine, hung with all sorts of votive offerings, with numerous lights burning in front of the figure of a *black* Virgin—an actual negro Madonna—decked out in very fine clothes, flowers, etc. This was *la Vierge noire*, or *Notre Dame sous terre*—a miraculous image which, ever since the Middle Ages, has been the object of profound veneration. How it originated, or what part it has played in the history of the town of Chartres, not being an archæologist, I can not tell. It was a very queer-looking thing, this image; one of those extraordinary mixtures of the pathetic and the ludicrous so constantly seen in Roman Catholic churches. In front of the funny black doll, two women—common peasant-women, of the class to whom it had been found necessary to interdict "*paniers, fardeaux, et chiens*"—knelt, absorbed in prayer, for ever so many minutes; then one of them rose and went toward a small erection hard by —a sort of shop-counter, behind which sat intrenched a young priest. She whispered to him, and he whispered back to her; then some little transaction passed between them like the sale of a ticket, and he dismissed her, accepting her respectful courtesy and her money with a condescending smile. Instantly he reabstracted himself from all mundane things, and buried himself fathom-deep in the leaves of his breviary. I have seen many Protestants make to themselves against all unpleasant human duties a barricade of their Bible—reading it forever, though, if they loved it as they profess to do, they must long since have known it by heart from Genesis to Revelation, and be able to say of it, as a faithful girl once said of her locked-up love-letter, "Oh, I don't need to read it; I can remember it all!" But I never saw even the most bigoted Bible-reader plunge at it in the ferociously sanctimonious way with which that young priest darted into the study of his breviary.

I hope it was an interesting work, but to me there would have been something far more interesting in two little works of nature which just then trotted past me, clinging desperately to their mother's two hands—an exceedingly poor mother; and the boy and girl with her were, like herself, almost in rags; yet she had arranged the rags tidily together, and come fearlessly to say her prayers in the magnificent cathedral. She was not afraid of it, nor of the *Vierge noire*. As soon as she came in sight of the image she made the two little things kneel down before it, and then knelt down herself between them for ever so many minutes, quite motionless. So were the children. Their little bare knees pressed uncomplainingly the cold stone floor, and the expression of their faces was of extreme awe as they looked at the lighted altar, and all its curious adornments. I wondered what they thought of it, these tiny creatures—one was three, and the other six, apparently; but, being so small and starved-looking, they might have been older.

I wondered, too, what their mother was thinking of, or praying for; and what sort of a home, if any, she had come from, or was going to; and what she hoped the *Vierge noire* would do for her. Probably the only thing she wanted was what all can not get, not even mothers—daily bread, mere daily bread—she had such a hungry face—and so came to ask it of her whom Protestants as well as Catholics somewhat profanely call "the mother of God." *She* could not hear, but God himself might, and answer too, in spite of the deluded and delusive prayers. It is a blessed thing to remember, amidst all our disputes about truth, our teaching and unteaching of it, and our vehement quarrels over one another's half-teaching and half-learning, that, through this maze of confusion, in His own silent, secret way, the one Divine Teacher is patiently instructing us all.

We left the woman praying, with her babes in front of her, close to the feet of the Black Virgin, and wandered away round and round the great, silent, solitary building. We went through nave, choir, chapels—there are seven—penetrating to the deserted high altar, and mounting inquisitively the empty pulpit—trying to feel as a preacher would feel who looked down from that eminence on the vast void below filled with eager faces —eager for what he had to tell them. Suppose—just suppose—for it must have often happened—that what he had to say he did not believe in himself?

Being neither architectural nor archæological, I do not attempt to describe the cathedral, but I can well imagine it is a treasure to antiquarians. There is, for instance, a screen of stone-work, composed of very well-sculptured reliefs—scenes from the New Testament history, which alone would occupy days of study. It was begun in the sixteenth century, and not finished for two hundred years. What generations after generations must have expended their life-long work upon it, and departed without even the hope of seeing it complete! Truly these workmen of the Middle Ages must have "died in faith," after having labored in faith, for their labor was of that delicate, careful, interminable kind of which they could never see the fruits. What a contrast to us—this impatient generation—hastening to be rich, and eager to spend our riches even before we get them; spending them, too, upon ourselves and our own personal luxuries—is the quiet patience, the solemn unfulfilled hope, in which must have lived and died these mediæval generations! Compare the men who build houses, "elegant mansions" and "desirable residences," splendid crumbling shams, meant to last only for a few years, with the men who used to build cathedrals!

We could have lingered for hours in this one, every stone of which preached a sermon—and all the better because there was no guide or guide-book, or intellectual interference of any kind with the purely spiritual influence of the place. But, in spite of the spirit, the flesh was weak; we began to feel frightfully hungry—thirsty too, as though we had been feeding on the dust of ages. As we went out, striving to find our way back into the town, and passed one by one those comfortable, respectable closed doors, whence grinned those easy-minded cherubs, and inside which we knew not a soul nor a soul knew us, our spirits began to sink a little. It is a queer sensation to be in a place so utterly strange that you feel your only reliance must be on the money in your pocket, if you happen to have it—but what if you have not? What will become of you then? We were libeling human nature. Let me, in contrition, tell the next episode.

We came to a little corner shop. It contained nothing eatable, drinkable, or purchasable, only coffee-berries, sugar, mustard, and such-like attractive condiments, so tantalizing to starving people, abundantly displayed. Still it was a shop, and in it sat a good-natured-looking woman. Despair gives courage: I went up to her and begged—with the apology of being "*étrangers*"—the stranger's charity—the immemorial "cup of cold water." She rose up at once, took us through the shop into the little back parlor, placed chairs for us, and with the sweetest, kindliest grace, went herself to fetch what I think was one of the purest, most delicious draughts that ever refreshed thirsty souls. She would have added wine to it, or bread, or any thing—indeed she urged this, and made us heartily welcome to sit and rest as long as ever we liked. We did stay some minutes in her neat parlor, talking about the town, cathedral, etc., and, as regarded the latter, being corrected in our moderate adjective "*grande*" by her earnest and rather reproving exclamation "*C'est magnifique!*" But when, in bidding her adieu, there was made the awkward and truly British suggestion of "something to pay," it was charming to see the air with which she drew herself up—this smiling little Frenchwoman—and the annihilating negative she put upon every thing but thanks, even accepting these with a dignified deprecation—"*Je ne merite pas.*" She has, doubtless, quite forgotten us, but we shall long remember her, and wish her, as we wished her on departing, the stranger's blessing, and the reward of those who give cheerfully a cup of cold water—which when I referred to I do not think she understood, Catholics being usually better acquainted with their Prayer-book than their Bibles: she only smiled sweetly, and looked after us with a kindly air. She did not know it, but she had done us good unawares.

In the Hôtel du Duc de Chartres we were entertained in no ducal manner: the *demi-poulet,* which seems to be a French waiter's first and last idea in the matter of extempore food, must have run upon its long legs for several summers, and the *mouton* was—well! let us forget it. But the *café au lait,* the bread and the butter, were, as they are all over France, excellent. And the neat-handed damsel who waited upon us, and got every thing as fast as she could, for we had no time to lose, was also thoroughly French in her quick way of divining our wants, and her cheerful, civil attention to them. She told us in summer Chartres is full of "*étrangers,*" but now we were evidently regarded as the first swallows of the season, and inspected accordingly.

Indeed we felt convinced that "*Anglais*" must be plainly written upon our exterior, for in passing through the market-square, and lingering at one of the booths, hoping to find, as a memorial gift to bring home to a friend, something a little less inconvenient than a saucepan, a frying-pan, or a three-legged stool, and trying to make the dealer comprehend what we wanted, we were painfully humiliated by a second man's coming up voluntarily to explain in a patronizing voice, "Yees, von franc—dat is tenpence." And when we praised his English, and inquired where he had learned it, he beamed all over with satisfaction, and informed us that he had been for a week at "Lonedone"—at the Great Exhibition. Then he began to dilate on all his experiences there, and the wonders he had seen—his companion listening with much respect, and evidently regarding him as a traveled personage—the monkey who had seen the world—who was, on the whole, rather a credit to his native Chartres.

Our small purchase completed, we again sauntered through the market, and stopped to watch, with considerable amusement, another business transaction of a much more serious kind. A grave old farmer was buying a horse, which the seller and a friend—a young fellow, having the peculiar sharp look which horse-dealers and all people who have much to do with horses seem to acquire—were trotting out before him, and urging upon him with a wild clatter of tongues, in which the only distinguishable word was "*garanti, garanti,*" repeated many times. But still the knowing old farmer shook his head, and after having felt the creature all over, and examined him with the eye of a connoisseur, he apparently declined the bargain, for the two young men marched their animal off, and themselves likewise, with a somewhat crestfallen air. I suppose even at Chartres there may be such a thing as a "do," and that there, as with us, people are not always so innocent as they look.

On again, through those quiet and half-empty streets, meeting only Chartres children with their *bonnes* going out for an afternoon walk; and Chartres ladies, dressed in all their best, going apparently to pay calls; and a barefooted, bareheaded Dominican friar, whose costume looked so queer contrasted with that of modern civilization, but who stood, indifferent to all observers, contemplating the cathedral front. For there, of course, we had drifted back, impelled by a kind of fascination.

It was the hour for vespers. From one of the great towers a deep-throated bell was sounding, and several very respectable-looking persons—chiefly women—were entering at the door. We entered too, and joined the thinly-sprinkled congregation which dotted here and there the enormous aisle, through which began to roll a sound not unlike the sound of the sea—bass voices, with violoncello accompaniment, singing the evening Litany. In the vast cathedral it seemed a mere murmur; and yet there was something at once fine and pathetic about it, as it swelled upward, wave-like, toward the great rose-windows, and lost itself in the mists of the almost unseen roof. It seemed to carry with it, as the sea does, the burden of the nations—the cries and prayers of centuries, that have beat themselves out moaning for a little while and vanished away. A mere human life—a generation of human lives—how very small it seems!

Outside the choir lingered one or two people—a few old women, whose *sabots* clattered faintly across the stone pavement, and one stout, middle-aged, very common-looking *père de famille*, who knelt down in a corner, and said his prayers with extreme devotion. Otherwise there was no sound but the low bass murmur of vespers, which seemed to make the rest of the cathedral more silent than before.

Vaguely wandering round it once more, in complete content of enjoyment, we came upon an *affiche*, which attracted the English Protestant mind as so "odd" that I stopped to copy it out. It was a printed paper, stuck on a pillar, and headed "*Sort spirituelle pour le soulagement des âmes du Purgatoire.*"

"*On dit ordinairement un de Profundis, un Pater, et un Ave, pour les âmes dont le chiffre répond au numéro sorti. Des personnes zélées ne laissent pas même sortir leurs amis de leur chambre avant d'avoir tirés un sort et dit Requiescat in Pace.*

"*Le bienheureux Jean d'Alberac adorant les Plaies de Jésus-Christ, pour les âmes du Purgatoire, vit qu'il en délivrait par ce moyen un si grand nombre qu'elles s'élevaient au ciel comme des étincelles d'une fournaise ardente.*"

Now I have no wish either to joke upon this rather peculiar *affiche*, or to recoil from it in frantic horror. I have not the slightest fear, nor, I trust, contempt, for the Pope or his Church; but I would just like to ask any sensible, sincere, large-minded Catholic, What does it all mean? Is this "*sort spirituelle*" a lottery for departed souls, in which the relatives of the deceased are to take tickets before the corpse is removed from the death-chamber? How are the said souls to benefit thereby, and for what length of time? and is the time proportioned to the money? Are the results guessed at, or calculated as we calculate averages in life-assurance tables? And will a proportion of the Catholic community in Chartres believe it, and pay? which fact one could understand of people like the woman with her two ragged children, or the good folk who come to church with the "*paniers, fardeaux, et chiens;*" but of the intelligent, educated people, who live in those comfortable houses, and send out those pretty, well-dressed children with their *bonnes*—those respectable middle classes of our nineteenth century—is it possible? Do they sincerely believe that, by paying so many shillings or pounds, the souls of their dead friends will be seen—as by the blessed Jean d'Alberac—(who in the wide world was that gentleman?)—"flying upward like sparks from a fiery furnace?"

I will allow there is something in human nature which clings to—nay, seems out of its own hopes to have created—the doctrine of Purgatory. It is a doctrine neither incredible nor impossible—within limits. Nay, I will go so far as to say that it is much easier, much more consonant with our highest idea of God, to believe in heaven and purgatory, or heaven and annihilation, than in heaven and hell—which one day may no Christian soul dare to believe in! And while human love remains so strong, and human creatures so weak—while the good, hating the sin, are continually yearning with a passion of pity and tenderness over the sinner—while there was never a lost life yet which some fond heart could not see excuses for, as none else but God could see—so long will there exist a craving after some sort of intermediate state after death, where all hope is not extinct, but in which the infinite number of souls who seem half good, half bad, who have fallen away under sore temptation, or succumbed to circumstances which they were born too weak to resist, may have another chance as it were, and be purged from evil, and educated through any amount of suffering into that ultimate perfect holiness which is the only real "salvation." It may be a most heretical thing to say, but I am sure there have been many men and women—women especially—who, could they have really believed in Purgatory, would have given their whole substance in masses for the dead, or spent half their existence in barefoot pilgrimages to shrine after shrine, praying for those departed souls, dear to them as their own, whom death had snatched from the possibility of attaining to good or atoning for evil in this world; leaving them, as their sole refuge and consolation, God's mercy and God's judgment—both, oh how far beyond and above man's!—in the world everlasting.

Yes, there are few of us who can not understand, and perhaps, in our secret hearts, even wish for, Purgatory, or something similar: it would heal so many wounds, clear up so many difficulties; but to suppose that we—or, above all, our purses—can influence it; that taking a lottery-ticket can lift our beloved out of that mysterious state of trial into the bosom of God! Well, many wise and good people have believed in many foolish and bad things; but still I should like to have caught one of those priests who sung their vespers so complacently, and asked him what the Catholic Church—no, the intelligent Catholic laity—really thinks on the subject.'

We had no time to ponder much upon it, serious as it was; for the afternoon was fast flying, and by evening we had to be present at a very different scene from this gray, sombre, silent cathedral. We walked round it once more, trying to view all its beauties from their several points, and fix them upon our minds as one does all delightful things that we know will return no more. This is the great regret of traveling—one feels as if one would like to stay in every pleasant place, as poor young Shelley used to say, "*forever*." One deludes one's self with the promise, "We will certainly come back again," conscious all the time that it is a delusion—that we never shall come back—that by-and-by we shall not even wish to come back; that, before we are aware, the "forever" has changed to "never;" and that, even if our own minds were constant to their first impressions—which they so seldom are—the eternal progression of things goes sweeping on, making our inconstancy unregretted —nay, almost unperceived.

We are never likely—perhaps should scarcely care— to see Chartres Cathedral again; but we feel glad to think that long after we are disembodied spirits, whom nobody will take lottery-tickets for, these lofty arches will lift themselves up toward the mist-clouds of the roof, and the lovely colored lights will tremble through the three wheel-windows, while down below the low monotonous murmur of vespers will go on day after day, and the poor old women will creep in and go clattering in their *sabots* over the pavement, and many a sick or sorrowful soul, of poor or rich—for both are alike with God —will come and lay its burden before the *Vierge noire*. But we shall have laid down all our burdens, done all our journeying, and entered into rest. And there comes a time—I am sure it does come in old age, and even before then—when that rest, which to youth is such a terror and dismay, seems as natural, right, and merciful as the nightly dropping of "tired eyelids over tired eyes."

Between the cathedral and the railway station we passed through a pleasant region, sloping down the low hillside on which the town sits to a place half rampart, half garden, where were trees, and gravel-walks, and seats, evidently a favorite promenade. There elderly gentlemen were turning out to take the air; and young ladies in jackets, hats, and chignons, and middle-aged ladies in bonnets and shawls, were wandering about. No doubt the society of the little old town, coming forth to amuse itself before dinner. We noticed their pleasant provincial look, and speculated on their domestic life—probably as simple and undistinguished as their appearance. Nay, we investigated it so far as to penetrate boldly through the open door of a *maison à louer*, where two merry young *menuisiers* were singing over some piece of carpenter's work, with a still more juvenile painter and decorator chiming in from his scaffolding inside.

This youth took the pains to inform us, with the utmost courtesy, and "Pardon, Madame," without end, that it was not the slightest use our applying for the house—which he evidently thought our errand—since, though it was still put up *à louer*, it was in reality sold to a family who were coming into it immediately. Nevertheless, Madame was quite free to go all over it as much as ever she liked. Yes, it was a very pretty house, and would soon be put into beautiful order, added the young workman, evidently gratified by its being admired.

So we went over room after room of this unknown home for some unknown family—doubtless as thorough-

ly a "family" as any of ours—perhaps more so—for in
French provincial life the domestic tie seems strangely
strong, stronger than we in England have any idea of.
The little domain was entered by a broad walk, dividing
a square, walled-in garden, where on either side were
flower-beds — some newly planted, some gay with cro-
cuses, violets, and red, yellow, and lilac primroses, which
looked as if they had rooted themselves there, and bloom-
ed spring after spring with a loving persistence, as faithful old-fashioned flowers do. On either side of the door
were the *salon* and the *salle à manger*—*Anglicè*, the two
parlors—prettily papered and freshly painted; behind
was the neatest little kitchen in the world. Above, a
queer narrow stair led to three tiny bedrooms, two facing
the front garden, and one the back, which latter was an
extraordinary specimen of horticulture, being a mere ter-
race-bank, ascended by a sort of step-ladder, and planted
with a few herbs and vegetables, such as would supply
the small *ménage* with materials for its *pot-au-feu*.

Every thing about the place was perfectly simple,
but so cosy, compact, self-contained, that the inhabitants
might live in it as snugly, as quietly, and as much to
themselves as birds in a nest, swinging safely on a tree-
top, out of every body's way; which always seemed to
me, in my childhood, the ideal of felicity. And then the
cathedral towers protecting them from behind and before, a sunny view of the smiling green *paysage*, sloping
down and then up again toward the horizon, dotted with
farm-houses, and intersected with rows of trees—what a
peaceful, happy life this family—it must be a small family—might lead there!—a life as unlike that of Paris as

our English provincial life is unlike London. We hoped it might be so, and we left our blessing behind us on these unknown people, for whom their "home" (and the French know what home is, though they have no word for it in their language) was so pleasantly preparing.

We almost envied them, for we had taken a liking to this quiet Chartres, and would gladly have spent a summer there—or many summers, perhaps—after the fashion of Shelley's "forever." But our hour was come— and our train. Before long we had left it all behind, and were whirling away back to Paris, which we found looking just as ever, though an interval enormous seemed to have come between us and it since nine in the morning. True, we had not done much—indeed I doubt if we had seen as much as we might, as most tourists would have seen. But all we had seen we had seen thoroughly, and as thoroughly felt and enjoyed, making of it a permanent picture, to go back upon for many a year.

Yes, we returned to Paris, and enjoyed it too, or made the best of it, which is the next wisest thing. But I am afraid, under all its splendors, and amusements, and dissipations, I left a little bit of my heart lying buried under the red primroses of that pretty garden belonging to the tiny *maison à louer* in the gray old town of Chartres.

G

CHAPTER VI.

WE FOUR IN NORMANDY.—PARIS.—CAEN.—BAYEUX.— ST. LO.

Foreign travel is like a tarantula bite—once beginning to dance, one must dance on. The exertion may be more painful than pleasurable, still we keep it up. The lookers-on—the quiet, phlegmatic, or selfish stayers at home—think us very foolish; perhaps we ourselves have our doubts whether we are not rather foolish too. Nevertheless we go dancing on, and dance until we die.

Thus it was not wonderful that, after a hard year of work, certain very hard-working people should, in the autumn of 1869, make up their minds to a mutual tour, to be recounted here under the title "We Four in Normandy." Who "we four" may be, and what are our personal characteristics, can not much signify to any body; therefore suffice it that we pass, like penitentiary prisoners, under our mere numbers—1, 2, 3, 4—Number One being a gentleman, and Numbers Two, Three, and Four of the inferior sex.

We started—not all together; Numbers Three and Four having left London a fortnight before, and spent their time at a sea-side village in Calvados, where, they wrote, the visitors, about seven in number, promenaded in bathing costume, and whiled away the intervals of dipping with the interesting amusement of shrimping. There was nothing much to see but sand, and hardly any thing to eat except shrimps. Yet they averred it was a charming place, and tried to tempt Numbers One and Two thither, but in vain. "The force of friendship could no farther go" than Caen, where a meeting was appointed on a certain happy Saturday.

But on the Friday night it blew a terrific gale. "We shall hear of wrecks to-morrow," cheerfully said the ticket-clerk, of whom a few inquiries were being made by Numbers One and Two as to the Southampton and Havre steamers. The couple looked at each other. A holiday was sweet, but life was sweeter. So they slept on shore, and next morning, in the temporary lull of a glorious September day, with the sea like glass, and the sky like an arch of lapis lazuli, they, blessing their own prudence in having changed their plan of route, embarked at Dover in the Calais boat for that brief crossing which seems such a trifle, but is—we know!

Alas! "how like a younker and a prodigal" do we every one of us start from those gleaming cliffs of Albion, and how soon does fate overtake us! I prefer to say nothing about that sunshiny crossing, with its delusive calm and long ground-swell, relic of last night's storm. Its most vivid recollection shall be a sweet human face—an old lady's face, for she must have been at least seventy; and yet I have rarely seen a countenance more beautiful—classically perfect, besides being mobile and expressive. She sat beside an old man in clerical dress—apparently her husband—until, benevolence rousing her, she went about from passenger to passenger, administering consolation and eau de Cologne in a way that showed how natural kindness was to her, and how she had probably spent her whole life in doing good to any body and every body she came near. I never found out her name; I have not the remotest idea who she was; but her kind smile, soft voice, and the touch of her hand are the pleasantest—the only pleasant—recollections of our first day of holiday.

In France again, and speeding along that dullest, ugliest of railway lines between Calais and Paris. No possible amusement outside, so let us try to find it inside the carriage, where is sure to be a little bit of human nature—always interesting—ay, even though three of our traveling companions are compatriots, and, as we soon detected, belonging to the most uninteresting class of that valuable but rather trying portion of the community who gain money first and education afterward. This worthy pair were not bad specimens of their kind; the man had a shrewd, intelligent face; the wife, if homely, was comely, and when she took out a magnificent lunch—a partridge well cooked and well cut up, peaches which made thirsty souls' mouths water to look at them; bread, salt, knives—nothing forgotten—and administered these dainties of her careful providing to husband and son, you felt that she was a good house-mother, thoughtful and kindly—ay, even though her *h*'s were deficient, her clothes resplendent, and her hands not so daintily kept as they might have been. Refinement and taste would come in the next generation—the ornamental superstructure over a sterling, sound foundation. One could guess this already from the face of the little son, who, we discovered, was going to a French school, armed with plenty of British courage and a bran-new British pocket-knife. This knife, evidently the delight of his heart, was the chief amusement of the journey. It slipped through a hole in the carriage window, and was thought to be lost forever, till, at Abbeville, an ingenious guard recovered it, to the unlimited ecstasy of the little lad, who, for all his pluck, had been as near crying as it was possible for a twelve-years-old Briton to allow himself to be in France, and had attracted the sympathy of not only ourselves, but of a sixth passenger—quite out of the pale of family life and interests—a French priest.

I have little liking for French priests in general. They are usually coarse and common-looking; good men, I believe, many of them are, but there are very few whom you could at all mistake for either clever men or gentlemen. This priest, however, was a striking exception. Thin, spare, sallow, with a good forehead, and a nervous, yet firm and expressive mouth, he was (if that gentleman will pardon the comparison) as like the portraits of the Rev. Charles Kingsley as if the Catholic priest and the Protestant canon had been twin-brothers — evidently a gentleman born and bred; something of the ascetic, a good deal of the scholar, and just a touch of what we call "the man of the world" — the old man (he was much older, I should observe, than his English "double") formed a most curious study.

He studied us in return. From under his thick brows, and over the top of his breviary, he watched all his fellow-passengers with the keenness of a man accustomed to observe life. At last he ventured a remark to the respectable tradesman opposite.

Vain courtesy! John Bull only shook his head; intimating with shyness and regret that he did not understand French, and hesitatingly offering a *Times*, which the priest eagerly accepted. In answer to a few words of French, ventured out of sheer benevolence by Number Two (who is gifted with that noble indifference to making a fool of herself, so valuable in foreign traveling), he explained that, though he could not speak English, he read it easily, and was much interested in England, having been there once for three or four days.

The ice thus broken, he seemed quite delighted, and dashed into conversation with true Gallic volubility, and that pleasant courtesy—such as trying to speak slowly, and never hesitating to repeat a sentence again and again till understood—in which we Britons might well copy our opposite neighbors.

The newspaper containing the daily bulletin of the Emperor's health, he being seriously ill just then, was the first obvious topic. "Suppose he should die, do you think there will be a republic?" was the question put, second-hand, by the two Englishmen—of course politicians—all Englishmen are.

The Frenchman looked over his shoulder with that instinctive movement of his countrymen when talking politics, as if there were a *gendarme* behind; and then recognizing that we were all Britons, risked an opinion. "A republic is not improbable—at least not impossible; but, even if established, it will not last long. Nothing with us now ever does last long. We French of to-day have ceased to be politicians. We are artists, authors, musicians, men of the world, men of pleasure. No, we are not *men* at all; we are mere children (*nous sommes en-*

fans), and, like children, we think of nothing but amusing ourselves. *La politique* is only a memory, belonging to the past generation."

Here Number Two hinted gently that Monsieur in his early life must have lived among a very different generation from the present, and seen a very different sort of France.

"*Oui, oui, oui, Madame,*" said he hastily, but offered no further answer, nor seemed at all inclined to enter, with the tender garrulity of age, upon the days and events of his youth. Yet they must have been striking, for he could not be far short of seventy, and in manners was distinctly what we should call in England "a gentleman of the old school." How far superior to the new I will not say.

Conversation now became decidedly interesting, and extended visibly. The priest's extreme courtesy, and Number One's quick intelligence, soon broke down the barrier of language, and, though one spoke little French and the other no English, they managed to make themselves comprehended in degree. He told us that he was *curé* of a parish in Paris—a fashionable *quartier*, containing almost no poor; which, I suppose, accounted for the fact that he spent his leisure hours in literature. He was shortly bringing out his first book—fancy a first book at the age of seventy!—and seemed as proud of it as if it had been an only child. We inquired its subject, and he told us it was "against Rationalism." Thereupon ensued a most curious conversation between the two earnest Protestants and the Catholic—equally in earnest, as one could plainly see—on the subject of this tide of unbelief, which is slowly overspreading France, England, the whole world. (N.B.—This being talk a little above the heads of the other good Britons, they retired from it, one into knitting and the other to newspapers.)

The priest was evidently well up in English affairs, political and religious. He spoke much about the members of his own Church among us—Newman, Manning, etc.—and was not ignorant concerning the great lights of ours, especially Dr. Pusey. He warmly admired our new Archbishop of Canterbury, Dr. Tait; and as hotly condemned a Frenchman whom he considered the common enemy of Catholic and Protestant faith — Renan. But he had a generous and appreciative word to say of an equal enemy of his, though not of ours, M. Guizot, the strongest opponent of Catholicism in France. Altogether this priest struck us as being a man of extraordinary liberal mind—for a priest; and once more we felt the never-ending wonder, how such a man could possibly believe his own creed.

His grand *bête noire* appeared to be this Rationalism, which, he averred, was corrupting French society to the core. "I fight against it," he said, "wherever I go; and I will fight against it by word and pen as long as I have breath." Was it with the clear, bright sword of Truth, or with the blunt weapon of dead Superstition, protected by the proof-armor of obstinate Dogmatism, which will not accept the fact that the world is a growing world still, in religion as in other things? At any rate, there was something at once noble and pathetic in the earnestness of the old man, defending his creed, alone, amidst strangers and—shall I say foes? No, we could not feel that. Priest as he was—bigoted Catholic as no doubt we should soon have discovered him to be—while we talked with him we felt only that he and we stood on the basis of a common Christianity. And when at last, quite worn out by his own energy and excitement, he dropped asleep in the corner of the carriage, and the tense muscles relaxed, and the flashing eyes closed, and the face became that of a tired old man, who would go to the grave alone, unwatched by wife or daughter, Number Two looked at it with a curiously tender compassion, though it was the face of a Roman Catholic priest.

Paris once more! In the whirl of the terminus disappear our worthy traveling companions, the English shopkeeper, his wife, and son. The French *curé* takes up his little valise, and, with a courteous bow to Madame, parts from us likewise, never to be met in this world again. Again the nocturnal blaze of the Rue de Rivoli and the murmur of the evening crowd circulating round and round the Palais Royal just as heretofore. And, next day, we start again; and that slow, lazy Chemin de fer de l'Ouest bears us through the not unfamiliar country —flat and unpicturesque, but wonderfully green and fresh —which first made us feel that Paris was not France, and that the whole of French scenery was not like that dreary line between it and Calais. Gradually the smiling pastures and rich cider-orchards tell us that we are in Normandy. The fruit is still ungathered, though a circle of blown-down apples lies at the foot of each tree, and the tall poplars in the hedge-rows keep swaying backward and forward in the angry wind.

Past Evreux, Lisieux, and other known places, all lying in the sunshine of the sweet Sunday morning, so peaceful, that we felt that quiet railway journey was almost as good as going to church; and then we stop at familiar Caen, and drive to the comfortable hôtel which we knew of old.

And here I find myself placed in a difficulty of conscience. In telling our adventures truthfully, "We Four in Normandy" shall require to say to the Normans a good many hard words, especially about hôtels. We meant at first, *pro bono publico*, to name the obnoxious ones; but it seems cowardly to abuse even a French innkeeper behind his back, and under circumstances where he can not even know of the attack, nor can possibly defend himself. I therefore prefer to keep the names of all the hotels we staid at under the shield of a merciful silence, excepting only that one which deserves the loving appreciative pre-eminence that I can not but give it. It is thoroughly French; English travelers expecting English luxuries will not find them: there are no carpets to the floor, and no spoons to the salt, and not a word except French will be understood in the whole house. But for simple, homely comfort and decency, for good feeding, attentive serving, moderate charges, and a general atmosphere of kindly civility, I know of no hôtel where I could so heartily wish to rest at, or stay at, as the Hôtel d'Angleterre, Caen.

And when, under its friendly archway, we saw emerging, full of joyous welcome, brown with sea-bathing, and "ironed out," so to speak, with the repose which even so brief a holiday gives to poor tired London faces, the familiar countenances of Numbers Three and Four, our cup of content was full.

Being Sunday, we of course made it as like Sunday as we could, by dressing ourselves as tidily as circumstances allowed, so as to appear a little less like tourists, and more like the respectable inhabitants of Caen going to vespers in Sunday bonnets and gowns. Number One, even, agonized by the truly John Bull necessity of a tall hat—without which it would be impossible to go to church—extracted his from its box, under the shadow of which glory we walked slowly to the Abbaye aux Dames, and "assisted" at the service—which possessed the great merit that you have not to assist, but may sit and think your own thoughts, and let your soul float quietly about the high arches, on the wings of the monotonous music, or, still more, the mere voice of the preacher in a foreign tongue. One may say what one likes against it, but there is great peace in going to church in a Catholic cathedral.

Peaceful, too, was our evening wander through the town, to see the solemn towers of the Abbaye aux Hommes stand up straight—bright and black in the moonlight, just as before—and feel that our pleasure in the quaint old town had not abated by absence. And pleasant the early rising of the following day, when we were to begin our tour in good earnest, by starting at 10 A.M. for Bayeux, but previously determined to see the celebrated "Marriage of the Virgin," and other noted pictures at the Hôtel de Ville. It was against orders, and out of lawful hours, but the plea "*Nous sommes étrangers*," put in the most bewitching of French by irresistible Number Four, together with a franc or two wisely administered by Number One, conquered every thing, and we entered. Now I have no wish to wound the feelings of the good folk of Caen respecting their treasure—a Perugino is, I suppose, a Perugino, and valuable accordingly; but after going through all the pictures, the thought came forcibly upon two of us at least, as it always does after traversing a collection, especially of old masters, that "*le jeu ne vaut pas la chandelle;*" and we quite agreed with a noted artist of our acquaintance, who once said, being asked to visit a gallery, "No, thank you; the truth is, I don't like pictures"—a feeling which, I am afraid, grows upon one as years advance. The only thing we do like is Nature.

We should have enjoyed studying Nature, and human nature, for a little longer, in the dear old town, but, afflicted with true British punctuality, we surrendered ourselves at ten precisely to the *salle d'attente,* to await the train from Paris to Bayeux. And there—we did wait! Certainly French folks take these things much more coolly than we do. One passenger, a man of business apparently, produced his pen and ink and paper, sat down, and wrote a heap of letters during his imprisonment. Another, a young priest, taking out a boy for a day's holiday—for we met both afterward in Bayeux Cathedral—waited dumbly for an hour, then, taking out his watch, meekly showed it to an official, and inquired when the train was likely to arrive. "*Je ne sais pas!*" was the answer, with a shrug; "but it will probably arrive some time." Fancy the feelings of a dozen expectant Britons waiting at Rugby for the Scotch mail, two hours overdue, and being told by a porter that it would probably arrive "some time!" So it did—just when even French patience was becoming exhausted, and English indignation was settling into silent despair; and nobody seemed the least astonished—nobody asked the smallest question. It was apparently quite an every-day occurrence. Our British wrath had scarcely subsided before we found ourselves at the journey's end—Bayeux, notable for its tapestry and its cathedral. In our minds, too, it will always remain notable for a third thing—the wildest and fiercest wind we ever met with in our lives —a gale which will long be remembered in Normandy, so great was the devastation it caused. It came westward from the Atlantic, and spread over the rich champaigns, sweeping them with the besom of destruction. The force of the blast was such that no ordinary trees could stand against it. The poplars bent, and let it pass over them; but the old, stiff, fruit-laden apple-trees were torn up by the roots, whirled about, and broken like straws. In the cider-orchards there was not a tree which was not maimed in some way, and many lay prostrate, hopelessly destroyed, the cows gathering round them, and feeding ecstatically upon the forbidden fruit; cows—Norman cows at any rate—being passionately fond of apples.

All this we noticed, half carelessly, as we swept along. It was not till we left the railway that we discovered how fierce the wind was. Walking felt like pressing against a stone wall; and as we went along, the tall trees which bordered the road were swaying to and fro like willow-withes. In the town—a quaint, sleepy old town, from which half the inhabitants seemed to have retired, and where we wandered along through the empty streets, munching delicious pears, of fabulously small price—in the town there was a little shelter; but when we got into the cathedral, it seemed as if a myriad of fiends were holding their jubilee overhead. The whistling, wailing, howling, high up in the lofty aisles, was something truly demoniacal—the more so for the bright sunshine without, and even within the cathedral, through which the wind kept up its invisible revels. It could do no damage—you felt sure of that—the strong pile was proof against its almost extremity of rage; you simply stood and listened, as you would to the roar of a distant battle-field, and thought what harm it might do—was surely doing somewhere—while you felt only a sense of pleasurable awe.

There is a family likeness running through all these French cathedrals. That of Bayeux is one of the finest; but I leave its description to Murray. The thing which most struck us, in noticing its wonderful perfection—perfect still—was the curious fact that these mediæval men, who must have lived, domestically, like pigs in a sty, as utterly ignorant of sanitary laws, or of the common luxuries and refinements of our day, as the beasts of the field, were yet able and willing to build for the worship of God these magnificent temples. Now we dwell in noble mansions, wherein we surround ourselves with every thing that art can supply of comfortable and beautiful; but—we build no cathedrals. Is that good or ill? Has our idea of God become diviner and more spiritualized, so that we feel we need not erect for Him temples made with hands? or have we sunk into a selfish, luxurious materialism, so that, provided we have our own snug houses to dwell in, we trouble ourselves little about the house of God?—a question which High-Church and Low-Church must decide between them. True Christianity lies apart from all these things.

Apart also from another phase of religion, which always seems to me rather more pathetic than ludicrous—the worship of relics. After wandering through these aisles, so grand and beautiful in their dim half-solitude, with the wind howling madly above our heads, we were taken into the sacristy, where, after exhibiting many curious things — ecclesiastical furniture dating from the thirteenth century, shown carelessly, as if of no interest at all—the old verger unlocked solemnly a gorgeous casket, and displayed, with intense veneration, three or four little black dots on a piece of silk or paper. These, he told us, in a low, awed voice, crossing himself devoutly, were a bit of the Virgin's veil, and the bones of several holy bishops. Truly, at that rate of minute distribution, one episcopal skeleton would supply the whole world with objects of veneration. We felt inclined to laugh, but would not, for the man had gray hairs, and evidently was quite in earnest. And, somehow, even a man who believes a lie, when he really does believe it, has something pathetic in his credulity.

So we passed on, abstaining from the shadow of a joke, and went out again into the streets of the ancient town, lying in the usual provincial peace, which to dwellers in metropolitan cities seems either enviable or intolerable. A great contrast, anyhow, to those stirring times which William the Conqueror's Matilda recorded in that curious monument of feminine diligence, imagination, and affection, the Bayeux tapestry.

Often as I had heard of it I had never thought much about it, and expected to see something quite different from that narrow strip of linen, scarcely more than a foot and a half broad, but extended on a frame, the whole length, up and down, of a very long room, upon which were sewed figures of the style of art of a boy's chalk designs on a wall, or a girl's of the last century on her sampler.

And yet Queen Matilda, if she executed this piece of needlework at all—which there is no reason to doubt—must have been a clever woman in her generation. Its exceeding variety—for as the canvas extends two hundred and fourteen feet, the scenes or pictures must be quite one hundred and fifty in number—the spirited conception of some of them, and the persistent care in the execution of the whole, do great credit to this queenly Norman wife—at once wife and queen. For the way in which she always depicts her William, front-face, while every body else is in profile, and the care with which his followers are drawn, armed and clothed, while our poor ancestors are represented as mere barbarians, sufficiently indicate that, like most historians, the fair chronicler was not as unbiased as she might have been, and knew well enough how to accommodate facts to opinions. Throughout, William is put forward as Britain's rightful heir (the first scene being his acknowledgment as such by Edward the Confessor), and Harold as a mean usurper. As the story goes on, the designer warms into enthusiasm, and the landing at Pevensey is quite an artistic success. True, the horses are blue and red alternately, and the men, who, except William, are all in profile, have a slight monotony of attitude; still the whole performance is interesting and intelligible, even to our modern eyes. Then, it must have been counted magnificent. The death of Harold, rude as the figures are, has a sort of pathos in it which the numerous " Findings of the body of Harold" that have tormented us in late exhibitions do not all possess; and the Gallic cock in the corner, crowing and flapping his wings in celebration of the event, is quite a stroke of genius. So, too, is the border, which at this point of the history changes its style, and, instead of being composed of irrelevant animals — supposed from Æsop's fables—is made up of slain men, in all sorts of possible and impossible attitudes.

Altogether no one can examine this curious work, especially where it breaks off abruptly, doubtless where the cunning of brain and fingers ceased, and the repose either of sickness or death fell upon a life that must have been anxious above most women's, even in those rough times —no one can think of Matilda in her individuality, which this labor of hers puts so strongly before one, without wondering what kind of lady she was; how she spent her days; whether she had a real, heart-warm love for that huge hero of hers, whose deeds she so carefully records—speculations idle enough, but almost as interesting as the tapestry.

Equally so, when we left it, was a bit of live humanity, contrasting with the dead archæology in which we had been burrowing for the last two hours. At the station was waiting one of the most beautiful persons that ever refreshed my sight. He was a young fellow, not above nineteen, but with one of those large, well-developed, well-proportioned frames, and high aquiline faces which one sometimes sees hereabouts, and which made one feel that the conquest of Britain by this grand Norman race was not such a very surprising thing. If the first Napoleon, who exhibited the Bayeux tapestry from town to town to stimulate modern Normans to a second invasion, could have also gathered together an army of such youths as these, it might have been, to say the least, a little awkward for us at home. As it was, we could regard this fine type of purely physical beauty with great content, wondering if Queen Matilda had among her sons any youths like him, and, if so, what a proud woman she must have been!

The afternoon light was fading over a lovely country, with fertile meadows like England, and glens just like Scotland, as we took our last bit of railway traveling to St. Lo, where the reign of locomotives ends, and that of *diligences* begins. It is a little town, set picturesquely on a hill-top: people told us there was "nothing to see" in it; but is there any place where there is nothing to see? I have ever since mourned over St. Lo, which we reached at dusk, and quitted at six next morning, feeling quite sure that it would have been worth remaining there at least a day or two, so charmingly "old-world" was the place, so quaint and kindly the inhabitants.

There was a landlady, the very face of whom tempted us to stay, instead of going on, as we first intended, to Coutances; and no other room being at the moment vacant, she established half of our tired quartette in her own. It was quite a picture. The furniture was mahogany, almost black with age; the hangings were of the pretty *crétonne*, which corresponds to our old-fashioned chintz. Beside one of the beds was a velvet *prie-dieu*, and over it a shelf, on which were arranged a number of religious ornaments. In a corner was a child's crib (Madame was still a young woman, with little children about her; but whether wife or widow, I do not know), and in the window-sill was fitted up an apartment, quite perfect in its way. There was a doll's toilette-table, a doll's chair, a doll's cradle; and in this cradle lay two young ladies (of wax), attired in blue blouses, like children, but boasting magnificent *chignons*. Every thing about these fortunate dolls was as complete as French taste and skill could make it. Numbers Three and Four were full of artistic admiration, and Number Two thought of her own little girl at home, to whom it would have been delightful to carry off the whole, even though, as usual at two years of age, total ruin of the treasure ensued within six hours.

Our *table d'hôte* dinner was most satisfactory and plentiful—in politeness. The *empressement* with which the *garçons* forced upon us an extraordinary dish—supposed to be liver (query, of what animal?) and beef, which I can only describe by the adjective *sanglant*—was amusing, if not appetizing. But after the bread soup, we felt no food to be safe till we came to the pears—huge, sweet Normandy pears—which, with a good piece of bread, were almost enough to dine upon—for a Frenchman. Undoubtedly we Britons rest far too much upon our beef and mutton, and suffer most ignominiously when deprived of them—as we did this day.

While looking forward anxiously to the *café au lait*,

and bread and butter, of which alone we could be quite sure, Numbers Two and Three being patient folk, and not exasperated by inevitable ills, sallied out to post some letters and arrange about the diligence journey of to-morrow. It was a still, clear night, and the quaint streets, dimly lighted by a new moon, looked most tempting. St. Lo was already on the point of retiring to rest; but we found one shop open, where a woman, with the charming politeness of the French middle class, nay, all classes, not only explained the way, but sent her little boy to show it to us. The small fellow trotted along by our side, chattering his pretty French, and as courteous and considerate as his elders—all for pure courtesy, too; for both he and his mother looked quite astonished at the gift of a few sous.

Equally polite, in that free way to which we are so unaccustomed in England, was the old man of whom we took places for the diligence. He explained with the greatest care what sort of vehicle it was, nay, even went out of his way to show it to us, and impressed upon us, with most fatherly anxiety, that we must take plenty of wraps, as it was sure to be very cold; also that it started at 6 A.M., and that we and our luggage must on no account be later than that hour at the bureau.

Consequently we hurried back, feeling that the one necessity of life was to go to bed at once, and try to forget our tired bones, our questionable dinner, and the uncertain prospect of the morrow in a good sound sleep—which we did.

CHAPTER VII.

ST. LO.—COUTANCES.—GRANVILLE.—AVRANCHES.

Does the establishment, the working staff, of a French hôtel ever go to bed? Are there any beds for it to go to? Or does it sleep surreptitiously on staircases, kitchen floors, or underneath *salle à manger* tables, crawling out thence when summoned, at any hour, ready to resume the never-ceasing round? We thought so when, being roused at 4 A.M. by the continuous clatter of *sabots* down the street—which meant the population of St. Lo going to its daily work in the dusk of the morning—we became nervously anxious about *café*, the *carte*, and the *diligence* at six, and at last descended to see if any body was stirring. No; all was solitude and desolation. In the dim court-yard a "boots," as he would be called in England, stood lazily gossiping with an outside friend; the kitchen, that ever-busy region, was empty and fireless; and even Madame's ubiquitous presence had vanished. However, in the space of ten minutes there she was, emerging from her charming bedroom, not exactly in the toilette of overnight, but wonderfully tidy, considering. *Café* appeared, excellent as usual. We ate, drank, settled our bill, saw our luggage away on the backs of two stout Normans, and in full, leisurely time, strolled down the gray drizzle of a decidedly autumn morning, to meet—whatever Fate had in store for us.

Diligences, like stage-coaches, are sure, by-and-by, to

drop into the sacred shadow of the past, their merits and "curiosities" remembered, their defects forgotten or ignored. Therefore we Four regret not that we took one day—a whole long, dreadful day—of diligence travelling. But we never mean to do it again.

Punctual to the minute, just as the clock of that picturesquely seated cathedral of St. Lo was striking six, we found ourselves at the bureau, and in face of a vehicle which would make any English coachman shiver. How that mountain of luggage was piled on to its shaky roof; how, once piled, it ever remained there without toppling over in the first twenty yards; how the horses were got into their harness, which seemed chiefly of rope, and so old that one would expect it to drop to pieces at the first strong pull; how, above all, any sane human beings would trust their lives and luggage to such a turn-out, was to us a marvel, and is so still. But the thing was done. We had chosen our destiny, and must meet it cheerfully—ay, cheerfully.

Of course the diligence did not start in time, and nobody seemed to expect that it should. Officials and passengers hung about, conversing lazily, sometimes lifting an accidental *malle*, or a bundle of reaping-hooks, or adding a market-basket to the heterogeneous mass behind the *banquette* (where we meant to sit; it was, at any rate, better than the *intérieure*); patting the patient horses; mending, after the primitive fashion with a bit of string, the harness, which seemed to be made for the great-grandfathers of the beasts before us, and used daily ever since. Yet every body seemed perfectly satisfied, and accepted, quite as a matter of course, the fact that it was nearly seven o'clock before there was the slightest attempt at starting.

At length we were desired, with the usual charming politeness, to ascend to our Siege Perilous, about as comfortable as the "knife-board" of an English omnibus, but certainly good for seeing the country—only, alas! there was no country to be seen. When, defended by waterproofs, hoods, and umbrellas, we looked about us, nobly resolved to enjoy ourselves, the little of the landscape that was visible seemed uninteresting to a degree. A long, straight, military road, stretching mile after mile without a single deflection, or any pretense of hill and dale; smooth pasture-fields on either hand, bounded by grass-dikes or hedges, with occasional trees, every one of which bore tokens of the violence of yesterday's storm—that was all. Now and then we passed a village—just half a dozen commonplace houses, of which one at least was sure to have its sign as a drinking-house—a bush of mistletoe hung over the door. To this were tied a number, greater or less, of apples, indicating, our *cocher* informed us, the price at which the cider within was to be sold.

"You drink cider entirely in this country?" one of us asked.

"Yes; and sometimes the apples fail, as they have failed miserably this year."

"Well, then you will have to drink water."

"*Ah! cela ne va pas bien,*" said our friend, with a melancholy shrug, which indicated that these misguided Frenchmen were as much wedded to their feeble, not to say nasty beverage, as our English laborers are to their adulterated unwholesome beer. But it was idle to preach, in either country, to listeners that would not hear.

Still, the ice once broken, our driver grew as conversational as his brethren of the whip usually are. He told us that he had driven along that road, between St. Lo and Coutances, for fifteen years, without missing a single day. Of course he knew every cottage he passed, and nearly every creature he met, and the number of greetings, jokes, messages, parcels, that he exchanged *en route* was endless. We forgot to admire the scenery—which, indeed, would have been rather a work of supererogation —in admiring him; his shrewd, bright, honest face, his ready wit, and his universal, genial politeness. Not at all the subservient respect of an Englishman; he evidently considered that he and his passengers were quite on a level, and could not be indifferent to his compliments to Number Four on her excellent French, or his personal sympathy with Number Two on her " *cheveux gris.*" And running his fingers through his own locks, he informed us the exact age at which they began to grizzle, how old he was now, and how many years he had been married, with the simplest confidence that all these facts must be to us of the most vital interest.

He had a shrewd wit too, honest man! When we noticed a flock of sheep tied two and two, he told us it was the custom of the country, to keep them from straying. " If free, they all go after one another—will leap through any thing, all in a body; but if thus tied, each wants to go a different way, and so they are safe and can't wander —like husband and wife, you know."

We also got at his sentiments on other points than

matrimony. Passing one village, we saw through an open cottage door several women and one or two men on their knees—the string of worshipers extending quite out into the road. He told us a woman lay dying, and the priest was administering extreme unction. "They think it helps them into heaven," added he, with a laugh and a wink at three passengers behind; workmen who, he had informed us, were going to finish the roof of a church a little beyond Coutances. These winked and laughed back again as at a well-understood joke.

A conversation ensued. With the help and interpretation of Number Four, whom even their strong *patois* did not daunt, we learned curiously and quite unwittingly the tone of religious, or, rather, irreligious feeling that exists nowadays among the French peasantry, of which these four were very fair specimens—steady, middle-aged, respectable-looking men; intelligent too, in a sense, though, to judge by the apple-hung mistletoe boughs, reading, writing, and arithmetic were probably at a discount among them.

We asked if the ceremony of extreme unction were common at dying beds.

"Universal. Nobody would be considered 'genteel' (that is the nearest English equivalent I can find to our friend's expression) without it. Anyhow, it does no harm. The women believe it does them good."

"But do *you* believe it?"

"*Ah ça!*" And the four men laughed at one another, evidently considering this a capital joke.

"They should have wives of their own—these priests—and then they would not come bothering ours. It is all their doing. Religion is for priests and women. We men are different."

"Then, when you come to die, of course you will not send for the priest?"

"Of course I shall! It is the fashion — *la mode*. One must do as one's neighbors do, or what would they say?"

So even here was the omnipresent Mrs. Grundy, driving people into Paradise the "genteelest" way. It was ludicrous, and yet sad too, judging by the half-cynical and wholly contemptuous expression of the honest peasant-face, as, a few minutes after, our driver took his hat off—quite civilly—to a fat priest whom we met. The shams which create shams—the superstition which necessarily begets skepticism—were only too plain; and one hardly wondered at the saying that in France all the women are devotees and all the men infidels.

While we had ceased to trouble ourselves about the scenery, the weather brightened, the landscape too, and in the distance we caught a glimpse of the Cathedral of Coutances, notable even among the many fine cathedrals in this part of France. In situation beautiful exceedingly, being built on the top of a conical hill, and visible in all directions. From its top, our driver told us, you could see the sea, with the island of Jersey, whence many people were in the habit of coming over, in summer time, to fairs and festivals—he often had his diligence crowded with *les Anglais*—on the strength of which he patronized us extremely, and took quite an affectionate farewell of us, when, after rumbling through the narrow streets, often with a vague dread that we might topple over into somebody's first-floor window, the diligence stopped at its bureau, and our journey was over.

But not our troubles. Instantly we were surrounded by a gnat-like swarm of aborigines, to whom the arrival of our vehicle seemed the grand event of the day. They buzzed about us in the most sanguinary manner, seeming resolved to pursue us to the death. Hand-bags, umbrellas, cloaks, had to be retained by main force from the persistent emissaries of different hôtels, each of which claimed us as their own. At last we allowed ourselves to be carried off by one determined young woman, who looked pleasanter than the rest, and decided our choice. That choice, alas! was a mistake; but—who knows?—the rest might have been equally bad.

We Four hereby solemnly caution any who are going to Coutances against stopping there. The five hours we spent in that dreadful town are still *un*-fragrant in our memories—and noses. Other towns, other hôtels, might have been worse—I think were worse; but this was our first experience, and it stands out in boldest relief, forcing on us the startling conviction that there are human beings even in civilized France to whom living in a pig-sty must be the normal and voluntary condition of existence.

But the cathedral was beautiful. Truly they were a wonderful race, the men who built these mediæval temples, which seem in truth not built, but grown, as natural a growth as that of the leafy arches to which they have so often been compared. Standing on the lowest of the winding galleries which run round the building, looking through it seemed like looking through some forest vista suddenly turned into stone. And then the loneliness of the place, broken by only one old woman, who told us—not very much of the cathedral certainly, but a great deal of her own innocent history, and questioned us as to ours. We seemed such wonderful creatures to have come all the way from London to see *her* cathedral, about whose grandeurs her weak, ignorant spirit flitted as harmlessly as a fly. When we asked any questions, historical or otherwise, she said " she would fetch her husband; perhaps he knew." But she herself knew nothing beyond having a certain vague awe for the place she was in, and a mild admiration—not for the solemn aisles, the lofty cluster-pillars, slender and graceful as pine-trees, the exquisite painted windows, forming combinations of color on which the eye reveled without end—but for some gayly-bedizened Virgin and Child, stuck in a tiny decked-out chapel, all frippery, and colored calico, and artificial flowers. One finds the same continually abroad, and the plunge from the sublime to the ridiculous is so sudden and complete that one gets to take it as a matter of course.

Could we ever take as a matter of course the filth, the squalor, the untidiness, the painful underside to all this beauty, which sometimes almost neutralized it? Was it wonderful that, when utterly wearied out, "sick in heart and sick in head," we sat waiting for the diligence that ought to have started at 3 P.M., but of course didn't? The cathedral itself was obliterated by its uncomfortable surroundings, and we felt that to get out of the hôtel and the town, to breathe free air, and catch the sea-coast view, which our map indicated, would be delicious.

But we reckoned without our host—or our fellow-passengers. Let me tell the tale, as a wholesome warning to diligence travelers.

We had taken our places early in the forenoon in the *banquette*, where we hoped for at least fresh air and a view of the country, and were just going to mount, when there pushed before us other claimants — three young priests and a layman. The latter, on our prior claim being represented, politely yielded. Not so those young fathers of the Church—rotund, jolly, "bumptious." The spiritual element, which, to judge by its fat cheeks and sensual mouths, had not at all let go of the temporal, could by no means condescend to be either " pitiful" or "courteous," or "esteem others better than itself," or any of those trifles which that true gentleman, Saint Paul, thought not unworthy also of a true Christian.

Deaf to remonstrances, they began to ascend, and would certainly have gained the day, and doomed us all to that smothering den among the luggage, where two men had already lighted their cigars, had not Number Four, besides her excellent French, been blessed with a clear sense, not only of other people's rights, but her own. With a mien firm and calm as Jeanne d'Arc's, she walked back into the bureau and confronted the official.

"These persons have seized upon our places, which I took and paid for this morning. You will please to return me my money."

"Mais, Madame—"

"It is useless discussing the matter. The diligence is just starting. Our places, or the money."

"If Madame will allow me to explain."

She stood calm, but remorseless as Fate, holding out her indignant hand. "Give me my money."

The official yielded. How could he not yield? Gabbling hurriedly, in some unintelligible *patois*, he rushed to the scene of action, and, somehow or other, in five minutes we found ourselves in our right places in the *banquette*, with the intrusive priests behind.

We had conquered; but we did not know our foes, who had the folly of boys and the rudeness of men. No sooner had the diligence started than they commenced a series of small annoyances, chiefly directed against Numbers Two and Four, who, fearing the combustible temperaments of One and Three, submitted meekly and silently to be elbowed, and pushed, and cramped, to have Coutances Cathedral—the last and loveliest view of it—completely blotted out by a huge, impertinent shoulder, and feel every breath of the fresh wind, which already had a taste of the salt Atlantic, contaminated by pestiferous tobacco-smoke. At last human nature could bear no more—the sufferers complained; Number Four in her most courteous French, Number Two in a patient silence that spoke volumes. One priest grinned, the other took no notice at all, the third stuck his tongue into his cheek, with a gesture that would have been insulting except that a boor always degrades, not the person he insults, but himself.

Then uprose the British lion and lioness in defense of their belongings. "Do that again, and you'll suffer for it!" "Serve you right, too, you—" Here Number Three paused for the worst term of opprobium she could find, and added, "priest!"

But the wrath fell harmless, seeing it was expressed in an unknown tongue. And the wronged parties, who had the "wise indifference of the wise," gradually succeeded in pacifying the other two. Also, since righteous anger speaks all languages, and the priests probably were cowards—most bullies are—they ceased their impertinences, and the rest of the journey passed in peace.

A curious journey it was, through a district that could scarcely be called beautiful, and yet there was a certain charm about it, an old-world grace, as if the face of the country had lain unaltered for centuries. In the villages, few and small, through which we drove, the whole population seemed to live out of doors; the women sitting sewing, the children playing round them. Now and then, in a hamlet of pretension, was a rope stretched across the street, with a lamp hanging in the middle; otherwise it was obvious that the inhabitants rose and went to bed with the sun, and that time, under the guidance of clocks and watches, was a thing quite unnecessary in these parts—a conclusion that experience forced upon us more and more.

Of course it was long after our fixed hour of arrival at Granville when a sudden glimpse of the sea implied that we were nearing that town. Hope of food and rest dawned upon us wearied and wayworn travelers. We drank in the pleasant evening breeze, and, tightly packed as we were, so that no one could well stir a foot without asking leave of the other three, tried to lean forward and see the sun dipping through a veil of greenish amber into the Atlantic, when up jumped the guard of the diligence, and said he must sit beside us. He had more than his legal complement of passengers, and, unless he could succeed in concealing one of them from the official eye, he would certainly be fined. So he explained—this not uncivil, big, blue-bloused Norman—and then, in the most good-natured way, he literally "sat upon" Number Three, extinguishing her entirely from public view, whistling meanwhile, with a cheerful nonchalance that would have deceived half a dozen government authorities. When the diligence stopped, and we descended, uncounted, he offered many apologies and thanks. But we had had enough. As that respectable vehicle disgorged us, and we stretched our stiffened limbs, thankful that we had reached our journey's end unharmed, I think each of us inly concluded that we had had enough of diligence-traveling to last us for the remainder of our lives.

Hark! actually an English tongue! It is a little bright-faced boy, who presses through the usual crowd which swarms round the diligence, and civilly suggests his hôtel as being the best in all Granville. We believe, and follow him. On the way he tells us his innocent little history—how he came over from Jersey some years ago, and is quite naturalized here—speaks English to all the English tourists, of which there are not many, and is very comfortable. He leads us through dark ways, and on through what looks like a back-kitchen door, to an old hostelry with queer passages, winding stairs, and in the very middle of it a court-yard open to the sky, which you have to cross on proceeding to your bedrooms.

Those bedrooms! Now our English hotel-keepers have many faults—are extortionate, careless, ill at cooking, worse at serving; but, as a rule, they are clean. We English are a clean people. We like to have things thorough. Even in laborers' cottages, of any decency whatever, you will find sleeping-rooms as tidy as the living-rooms; and in the commonest country inns, where the accommodation is of the plainest kind, with scarcely even a parlor to sit down in, you will find bedrooms where the coarse sheets are white as snow, where every thing smells of sweet lavender, and the floor is so clean you might " eat your dinner off it." Now these floors!—

When we quitted the *salle à manger*—a grand room, resplendent with mirrors and gilding, where a capital *table d'hôte* was going on—and went up the narrow, dark, dirty staircase into chambers deficient of every comfort, and which seemed never to have seen soap, water, and scouring-brushes for at least ten years, we shuddered! We decent English could not understand the anomaly. "Have you nothing better than this?" we asked.

Why, these were the very best rooms, the "English" wing, especially adapted for English tastes. (What must French tastes be?) Landlady and *femme de chambre* were alike astonished that we did not find every thing perfect—that the first room, which opened on a back street redolent of all ill odors, and the second, which, being just over the kitchen, was like sleeping in a frying-pan within scent of all the other frying-pans, were not considered paradises of repose.

Well, there was no help for it. We must sleep somewhere. So we retired, and, half roasted, half suffocated, spent a night of lively misery, listening to the moan of the sea—the only pleasant thing—and about 3 A.M. to a great commotion below—the departure of a number of travelers by the early boat to Jersey. It was blowing and raining so fearfully that we took a certain wicked consolation in thinking how very miserable they all would be —worse even than ourselves. And then a dreamy sleep came over us, just enough to separate yesterday from to-day, and give a sensation of its being properly morning.

Are we "enjoying" ourselves? was the mute question which I think every one of us would have put, and nobody liked to answer. On a tour it is a matter of conscience that you *should* enjoy yourself, and never breathe, even in your inmost soul, the not unfrequent sigh, "Oh, I wish I were at home!" So, when we looked out upon the dull gray town, struggling up the hill-side year by year in its attempts to grow from a fishing-village to a sea-bathing place, and then turned away toward the sea, equally dull and gray in the rainy morning, we tried to say how pleasant it was to smell the salt air, and what amusing *contretemps,* such as the night's disasters, one was always meeting in Continental traveling. And we planned to see all the sights of Granville, no doubt a very curious and interesting place, only we all agreed to get out of it as soon as possible. So, a carriage being arranged for—no more diligences!—we sallied forth.

Granville has one feature—a magnificent pier. It was begun in 1828, and is scarcely finished still. In its circuit it incloses a much older building, and it stretches out far away into the sea—a sea which it would have been delicious to gaze upon, raging and tossing as it was, in stormy wind and wild-beating rain, only you can not quite enjoy the picturesque when you feel yourselves slowly soaking, and have no clothes but those you stand in. And here for another word of warning. Having been beforetime overburdened with luggage, we now had determined to leave it all behind; and, armed only with bags, we meant to travel lightly and airily, with all our worldly possessions in our right hands. Fatal mistake! which we already began to rue. So, curious as Granville may be, fine the view from it landward and seaward (I believe the island of Jersey, thirty-three miles off, being the prominent object), our chief recollections of it are that wretched night, and a morning spent half in sheltering in a sentry-box from the torrents of rain, and half in drying ourselves in the *cuisine* of the hôtel, where the *cuisinier*, a most polite young Frenchman, with the dandiest little white cap on his head, cooked us successfully, turning us round and round at the fire as carefully as if we had been pigeons.

It is best to laugh at misfortunes, at least afterward; and we were in by no means melancholy mood when, under a blink of unexpected sunshine, we drove through the town, our horses' bells ringing cheerily, and our driver's voice also, as he "sang out" to all he met that he was going to Avranches, and was determined to beat the diligence, though it had started an hour before him.

He was a charioteer quite different from our other two. Our second diligence-driver had been a weak man, of silent tongue and quiet countenance; a domestic character probably, for on descending in one village he was embraced by two very ugly women, whom he kissed on both cheeks, for the public benefit, in the tenderest manner possible. But this third man was an altogether jolly rather than a sentimental person, and his chief affection seemed to be for his dog—a splendid bull mastiff, who ran after the carriage.

"He is muzzled, you see, Madame,- else he would strangle any body; he has tried it several times upon other people, but he is just like a lamb with me. Here," calling him by some unintelligible name, "*courez, courez —vite! s'il vous plait.*" (He always said "*s'il vous plait*" in the politest manner whenever he addressed this redoubtable animal.")

We won the master's heart by warmly appreciating the dog, and he drove us his very best—up hill, down dale, with an apparent recklessness, but real skill, which was most inspiriting. The land seemed to lie in waves, rising and falling, cut up into fields, chiefly of buckwheat and hemp. The road we went along was another of those perfectly straight military roads, traceable for miles before and behind, which are the characteristics of this district. It was bordered by hedges, on which hung —oh! such blackberries! If we could have stopped for them!—but no, Avranches was miles still away, and some of us were weary already. Still, it is one of the pleasantest bits to remember in our tour that long dreamy drive, in the unexpected sunshine, through a region which, if not beautiful, had at least the charm of novelty—past villages where life went on—quite a different life from ours, yet as vivid in its interests, as strong in its loves. It flitted by us, a mere painted panorama, through which occasionally a figure moved—peasants on foot or in rude carts; and, always saluted with much respect, passed singly or in twos and threes those sombre figures, with their womanish frocks floating behind them, and their shovel-hats shading faces sometimes young, sometimes old, but generally coarse, dull, and common-looking, whom Number Three, still burning under our yesterday's wrong, indignantly called "black beetles." They certainly seemed to be crawling about every where; and when one has imbibed a decided prejudice, how one is apt to assimilate all facts thereto!

Still, one thing must be allowed—that in France the apostolic successors of Him whom good old Dekker quaintly calls "the first true gentleman that ever breathed" are, as a rule, *not* gentlemen. The emoluments of the Catholic clergy are so small, its social status so low, that it is chiefly filled up from the peasant class—people to whom a son or brother in the priesthood is considered a great honor and pride. Consequently, many of them are ill-educated, unrefined, scarcely a whit better than their working brethren; probably inferior, as their lazy lives, and the slight veneering which their ecclesiastical teaching produces, may well give a surface polish and no more. At least this was the explanation offered to us, by good authority, of the fact, which we could not help noticing—the great difference, even socially, between the priesthood here and our clergy at home.

But we tried not to think about them, or about any thing except present pleasure—that truest wisdom of travelers, to snatch the passing joy as it flies!—when, after traversing miles upon miles of this long, straight road, and seeing from every eminence wide tracts of forest-country, green and undulating, which, a century or two ago, must have been glorious hunting-ground for nobles and kings, we began to catch, on the right hand, glimpses of the sea, shining like a great, glittering eye, and rising out of it, in the centre of a fine bay, one conical castellated rock, the primary object of our tour, which for years we had longed to see—Mont. St. Michel.

"There it is!" we all cried at once. "That is certainly Mont St. Michel!"

Yes—our *cocher* confirmed the fact, though without taking much interest in it. Many people went to see the place, and you could easily get to it across the sands from Pontorson, or by another way — shorter, though more difficult. All English people, he averred, thought a great deal of Mont St. Michel.

Every thing seen looks less grand than things unseen; and yet there was a wonderful majesty in this lonely rock, dedicated to the angel of high places, which has been successively a pagan temple, a hermit's cell, an almost impregnable fortress, a church, a convent, a prison, and is now a monastery once more. Oh, the stories it could tell of the conquering kings who held their courts here—of the pilgrims who thronged to its shrine—of the captives who languished in its awful *oubliettes!* But presently we shall take a whole day and see it—the goal of all our hopes, the object of our journey; so now we will just glance at it, standing mysterious in its lonely bay, with the afternoon sun shining on its granite points, natural or artificial; for the building and the rock itself are of the same stone. Then we lose sight of it, and come into a long avenue—for either side of the road is bordered with chestnuts magnificently grown—through which we pass to the foot of the green-rounded hill, dotted with many trees, that seem walking up and down its smooth curves like the elfin-trees of German folk-lore. At the top of it, like a lady from her castle-tower, looks smiling the pretty town of Avranches.

Every body had told us it was pretty, but not nearly how pretty it was. As we wound up the spiral road, gaining gradually higher and higher views of the forest-country on one hand, and the sea, with St. Michel on the bay, and the island of Tombelcine lying out like a great whale in the distance, on the other, we thought we had never beheld a lovelier place—one where weary souls might take refuge in, and find in the wonderful beauty of nature comfort against the ugliness of life's narrow but gnawing cares, that eat one's heart out before one knows it.

And when we dismissed our equipage, and bade a quite regretful adieu to our *cocher*—who, strange to say, was not merely satisfied, but grateful, for his pay and his *pour-boire*—and entered the hôtel—old-fashioned and simple, for you passed right from the street into the *salle à manger*, so that the *table d'hôte* was plainly visible to the whole town—what bliss it was to find rooms fresh, sweet-smelling, clean—yes, actually clean!—with their pretty chintz hangings and muslin toilet-tables reflected in their polished, dustless floors!

"Oh, let us stop here! Don't let us go any where else," was the anxious cry, especially of Number Two, who found herself slowly collapsing under the trials of Continental traveling. So we staid.

And pleasant—even when three out of us four had started off to investigate the curiosities of the town—very pleasant was it to rest idly in that shut-in hôtel-garden, the trees of which showed that it must have been a cultivated garden for nearly two centuries. Their leaves, still green and bright, quivered in the sunshine, overshadowing square walks that glowed with china-asters, African marigolds, zinnias, and other brilliant autumn flowers. Behind these, trained on espaliers, was most magnificent fruit—plums that made one's mouth water, and pears such as one only sees in Normandy. They hung so close to the hand, they lay so temptingly on the ground, that nothing but the strongest sense of *meum* and *tuum* could keep one in the path of virtue—that is to say, the garden-walk. Excepting that the birds were all dumb, and there was, besides the perfume of fruit, that vague autumnal odor which always carries with it a certain sadness—

"The faint rich smell of rotting leaves"—

that solitary inn-garden would have been a little Paradise. Only, perhaps, in Paradise one's limbs will not ache, nor one's head feel heavy and dull, and one will not have that intense longing to lay them down at peace on the familiar home pillow—closing one's eyes even to pleasantness, and only desiring rest.

Still, not despisable by any means was that comfortable chamber, its pale chintz, of which the pattern is vividly remembered still—a group of roses, with two birds stooping to kiss one another—and, set like a picture in the frame of the window, the gray roof of the opposite house, with its green *jalousies;* below which, in staring letters, was one half the name of its occupant, puzzling a sickly fancy to try and find out the other half; while, rising up from the world below, came, subdued into not unpleasant monotony, the high, shrill French voices of the passers-by, the tinkle, tinkle, tinkle of the horses' bells—(all horses seem to carry bells hereabouts; our *cocher* told us they would not go a step without them; what cheerful-minded animals they must be!)—and, lastly, the clatter of the wooden *sabots* down the street, which seems the perpetual undertone of all French towns.

Yes, yes, it was very peaceful; nay, to use a truly English word, of which we were fast forgetting the meaning, it was "comfortable." Things might have been better, certainly, but they might have been a deal worse. So, not lamenting uselessly the sweet temptations of the sunset—and the sun must be setting so gloriously just over Mont St. Michel!—or the moonlight—a real harvest moon, which threw the inn-garden into the grandest shadows, the most ethereal lights—we all gayly separated, declaring that we would take our grand excursion, our day of days, at Mont St. Michel to-morrow.

CHAPTER VIII.

MONT ST. MICHEL.

"The best laid schemes of mice and men
Gang aft agee."

ALAS! they do; and there is no fighting against the inevitable. Still, it was hard—and every month that the fact recedes into the past, convincing one more and more of its utter irremediableness, it grows harder—that after having longed to see Mont St. Michel for years and years; after having come all the way from London to see it, and see it in company with three other pairs of eyes which would equally have enjoyed the sight and enhanced its pleasure—to have to give this all up—and, aware that on no other possible day could the expedition be taken, to say calmly "Never mind. Go without me. I shall hear all about it second-hand, and this will be"— with an internal choke of disappointment—"this will be nearly as good."

But one can not tell about a thing second-hand; and the wonders of the place were such that, to half describe, or unworthily describe, would be perfect sacrilege. So here Number Two lays down her pen, and it is taken up by Number Four, who with her eyes beheld, and with her mind appreciated, every incident of that most interesting day.

Unfortunately, there could be no mistake as to the fact

of Number Two's illness. There was no help for it but that she must rest, and that on the very day fixed for our excursion to Mont St. Michel. She would not allow us to alter or modify plans so as to defer this visit until such time as she could accompany us; and there was no gainsaying her wish, as she said, "to subside." As this was the one expedition on which she had particularly set her heart, it was very hard for us to go without her; all the harder, because she insisted that it was very easy for her to stay behind. She "subsided" in such a patient and cheerful manner that we felt particularly depressed and guilty when we set out without her. I must say that she had a certain advantage in being sustained by the consciousness of self-sacrifice; we, of course, had no moral support of that kind, and when she bade us a heroic farewell, we slunk out, feeling mean and selfish.

If it has been borne in upon the reader's mind that we Four in Normandy were unanimous in our views, I must, with regret, correct that impression. We differed considerably on many points; and if we hadn't, I am sure we should have bored one another immensely.

For example, Number Four thinks Avranches one of the very dullest places she ever entered. Whether the English people who inhabit it found it dull, or have made it dull, or in what proportion their influence has affected it, she can not pretend to say. But it certainly was a cheerful thing to get out of it, even without Number Two, and with a sulky driver and two dejected horses.

Avranches is a city set upon a hill, and we descended the long steep slope by which we got away from it in silence. The road to Pontorson lay straight before us, or rather it seemed to rise up before us like a tall white column. On our right hand the sea had crept in almost to our feet, and we could trace the whole outline of the great bay which it has formed in the coast of Brittany and Normandy. A belt of tamarisks was in many parts all that separated the waste of sands that was dry land from the even more dreary waste of sands which was sea. But the shores of the bay were in some parts more picturesque, and we could descry green fields, and fine trees, and a rocky coast in the distance. At low tide the sands of the bay are dry, like those of Morecambe Bay in Westmoreland, but gray instead of golden, and in the middle of the bay two great rocks, steep and abrupt, rise from the level sands. They are about a mile apart. One is bare and uninhabited, and crouches low like a beast of prey; the other towers up to a lofty height, is surrounded by strong walls, and studded with houses from base to summit, and crowned on the very peak of the rock by a church. Both islands—for these are Tombelcine and Mont St. Michel—are surrounded by water at high tide, and even at low tide the gray level sands, with the ripple in them, give the effect of sea on a cloudy day.

We were to drive to a spot where the distance from the main land to Mont St. Michel is shortest, and where the sands are firm enough for a carriage to pass over them. Our way at first lay through green lanes with high hedges, from which the blackberries hung in great heavy bunches. We said, "If Number Two had been here she would have made us walk along these lanes; she can not resist ripe blackberries." We said it with a consciousness of superiority to weakness, and it was with a sense of condescending to weakness that we exclaimed from time to time, "What a pity she can not see them! We could well spare half an hour to saunter through these lanes, and they would make her as happy as a child." It is a very remarkable thing, and I can not account for it, but certainly, as we watched those hedges, the black bunches seemed to grow larger, and blacker, and more numerous, while the sunlight was more sunny, and the dust became dustier every moment. A "happy thought" occurred to Number Four. "Don't you think we might taste the blackberries, just to tell Number Two about them? It is so much easier to describe a sensation when you have really experienced it, and blackberries belong to such a remote period of one's existence." We all descended with considerable alacrity; Number Three, in whom the instincts of her youth will never be extinguished, took a stick with a large handle, made her way through the hedge, and soon returned laden with heavy boughs dropping black, sweet stains. She triumphantly compared them with our dusty handfuls, and proudly divided her spoils. We found that it would be impossible to take any of these back to Avranches, and so ate them " to the health of Number Two." And as we were eating a great stillness came upon us, and we forgot the sweetness, and the sunny lanes, and the pleasant land of France, and were carried back—at least one of us was—to English lanes of many, many years ago; lanes that are now terraces and squares of brick houses, that have left the region of youth and poetry, and are grown hard and gray; and the magic berries brought back young faces and happy voices—alas! the faces have become very grave, the voices sad and low, and some of them are altogether silent.

We were roused from our reveries by passing a barn near the road-side, outside of which three women and a man were thrashing corn. They stood as if for a quadrille, and the blows of their flails fell with unerring regularity.

The physical inferiority of women does not seem to be so strongly felt in France as in England, and if the men have any theories on the subject, they do not allow them to interfere with their practice of assigning a great deal of hard outdoor work to women.

While we were shrimping on the coast of Normandy, as described by Number Two, our luggage had one day to be carried for more than a mile before we reached a road passable for any vehicle. Our porters were a man and a woman, and it is therefore of no use to try and conceal the fact that we did not share Number Two's enthusiasm for a "hand-bag." In fact, we had each a large box, as well as a goodly number of rugs and shawls. The man, a great strong Norman peasant, took the lightest and easiest box, and left the little sturdy woman to toil after him with a heavy load. I overtook him and remonstrated: "How can you leave Jeanne so much to carry? You ought to take the largest share yourself, for men are much stronger than women." "Pardon, Mademoiselle. Most women are much stronger than men."

Soon we had lost the sight and sound of the thrashers, and the thoughts they gave rise to. Green lanes, and farm-houses, and barns were at an end, and our road lay by the sea, and with Mont St. Michel in view. We saw it for a moment only, and then heavy clouds closed over it, and wind and rain beat against us.

We passed over as bad a thing to be called a road as well could be—an uneven sandy track washed into furrows and ridges by the high tide, which had here and there left deep pools of salt water. The horses plunged and stumbled, and we had enough to do to keep our seats. This track must have been lost if it had not been for a hedge of green tamarisks on each side of it, covered, when we passed, with delicate feathery blossom. On the other side of the hedge a coarse and scanty grass was growing on the sandy soil, which was divided into square patches by ditches full of slimy stagnant water. Every now and then we saw two sheep, tied together by the head, dragging in opposite directions, one in a ditch, the other half way up a bank. In some cases incessant contention seemed to have paralyzed their efforts, and they were standing stock still—as far apart as the cord which united them would allow. After a time we came upon a gaunt, barelegged and bareheaded old woman, clothed in scanty rags, herding a cow. She held the lean beast by a cord tied to the horns, and was much tormented by its efforts to reach the reedy grass, and get away from the sand-bank on which she sat knitting.

The rain was over, and the sun shone again so that we could see Mont St. Michel clearly. The walls, ramparts, and houses round the base of the island looked as if they had been quarried out of the stone; above them rose the bare perpendicular rock with one yawning black mouth, from which depended an iron tramway.

"The prisoners worked there," said our driver, with sudden interest. "There is a great wheel inside, and they were shut up in the wheel, and had to tread it round and draw up provisions from beneath."

We strained our eyes to see the wheel, for the sunlight had shown dim forms, which we took to be a gibbet with ghastly figures hanging from it. Higher up we could see the walls again, and on the summit the church with its square tower.

Formerly, instead of a tower there was a spire to the church, and on the top of it a gilded statue of the Archangel, St. Michael, with a drawn sword held high above his head. This statue turned round upon a pivot, and was moved by the wind. Travelers, in former times, have described how, as they were crossing the sands from Pontorson when the sun was sinking in the west, the form of the Archangel would stand out dark against the fiery disk which glowed behind him, and surrounded him with a halo of golden rays, ready either to ascend to the throne of God or to come down and execute judgment upon earth, standing silent and dark while the sunlight leaped and flashed along the living sword. They tell how, in the storms and tempests of that region, the movements of the Archangel, and the gleaming of the great sword through the murky air, made men's hearts fail them for fear.

There is no Archangel now, and that yawning blackness in the rock has left ineffaceable traces of crime and punishment, of suffering and injustice. The prison has obliterated the priest, we thought, but a sudden turn brought us back to more immediate interests. We jolted over loose masses of stone, the ruins of a house washed down some years ago in a storm, and turned to cross the bay. It was low tide, and the sands were bare and dry for miles around and before us. They are greenish-gray in color, like London mud hard baked—so hard where we crossed that the horses' feet and carriage wheels made no more impression on them than they would on a good road. It is never safe, however, to leave the tracks marked out by conveyances which cross daily, as some parts of the sands are often suddenly transformed into dangerous quicksands, in which many imprudent travelers have lost their lives.

The little river Coesnon, which divides Normandy from Brittany, flows through the bay till it meets the sea. Now, at low tide, the narrow, shallow stream seemed to be losing itself in the sand. Here and there, at intervals, the bleached timbers of a boat, more than half covered and swallowed by the sands, told of wreck where there was apparently so little danger.

A diligence with four horses was crawling over from Pontorson to St. Michel, and there were a few people on foot, and two or three barelegged men fishing in the Coesnon. There was just enough life to make you feel what a wide and empty place it was, and how desolate.

We were close to the granite rock which guards the bay, and had to splash through the Coesnon, which flows partly round the island; then a struggle up the sandy bank, with many shouts to the horses as they reach the stone causeway, and we clatter through the one entrance into the island. We pass gate after gate, for there are three of them in the strong walls that protect the land-

I

ward side, which is not inaccessible like the side facing the open sea. We enter a street narrow and steep, with ramparts to the right and houses on the left, so close to the rock that they seem hewn out of it, and almost immediately we are at the door of an inn. A tall, gaunt brigand rushes forward and takes possession of us. I have reason to believe that I am not describing him accurately when I call him a brigand. I am assured that he is an amiable and kind-hearted man, a very storehouse of "sweetness and light," but the effect he produced upon us was that of a brigand—a brigand with ragged breeches which do not reach his knees, bare feet, and very hairy legs; his brown arms are also quite bare, and his head has no covering but its thick black locks. Perhaps it may be as well to state what he had, as well as what he had not, and that, in addition to the breeches, he wore an old sleeveless knitted vest, and a crimson scarf round his waist. He snatched our bags, rugs, and umbrellas from the wagonette, and, addressing us as his "*petit monsieur*" and his "*bonnes petites dames*," signified his intention of giving us in charge to a friend of his—a dear friend—who would look after us while we were on the island. He points to his friend, who sits crooning on a stone with a basket of shells and bead-work for sale.

We decide upon resistance; and having very clear views about what we should call luncheon in England and breakfast in France, we pass through the open doorway of the inn, and enter a low, dark room.

Two or three women are cooking at a large open fireplace: some drivers, who have come with other visitors, are eating and drinking at a large wooden table, dark with age and dirt. There is one window, which opens into the narrow street, and in it are glass cases full of shells and rosaries, and trifles carved in wood and bone. We pass to an inner room, and forget the brigand, and the promises which sound like threats, in the discussion of excellent omelettes, cutlets, and grapes.

The inn may be taken as a sample of most of the houses on the island. It is built against the rock, out of which the stairs and some of the rooms are hollowed. The stairs are so dark and gloomy that it seems as if they would lead to a dungeon; and the bedroom, dismal as it is, is quite a surprise. But there are ominous holes in the floor, and so many suggestions of rats, that we think with a shudder of a night spent on the island which we had at one time contemplated.

We leave the inn, and, to the disgust of the brigand, decline guidance and the regular walk round the walls. We resolve to climb the steps which we see winding up by the side of houses and little terrace-gardens, to take our own time and our own way, and go up and up as far as one can see, high up the rock, and to the abbey gates. Climbing and resting, scorched by the sun, and beaten backward by a fierce wind from the sea, which blew over the island, and struck us in the face, we reached the last flight of steps. The great walls and gates frowned above us as we sat down to rest and to look about us. The steps were not much used; tufts of grass and nettles grew in every crevice, with pellitory of the wall, and "blue flowering borage, the Aleppo sort."

Beneath us was the parish church, and its grave-yard, a small, narrow slip of ground on the surface of the rock;

a few slender poplars grew outside the wall which surrounded it, a large bay-tree flourished within, and there were many of the light iron and gilt crosses which one sees in all French cemeteries.

Steep, narrow steps led down to the church, which a priest, with two attendants carrying black vestments, were descending. They had pleasant voices, and were talking and laughing. The bright sunlight fell on them, and seemed to fall on the sounds also, and it touched the gilt crosses beneath them, and led the eye on over the houses and the sands to the bare island of Tombeleine—very gaunt and prosaic in such a bright glow; and then on again to the main land, with its happy fields, and trees, and villages, and Avranches standing high upon the hill, where we knew that Number Two would be rejoicing in the sunlight for our sakes.

But during this time the chapel bell was tolling; and we thought that, for all the cheery voices of the priests and the glad bright day, there must be sad hearts near us. Number Three has such a large sympathy with sorrow as well as gladness, that she could not go on to see the abbey while others were laying away their dead, but must wait reverently until the ceremony was ended. Number Four thought it as well to be certain of facts before lavishing sympathy, and so, descending in the footsteps of the priests, found that, as matter of fact, the church bell was tolling for the convenience of certain nuns, the roof of whose convent is on a level with the church-yard wall, and made signs to relieve the mind of Number Three. She then entered the village church, which, like all other habitations in the island, is built both upon the rock and against the rock, and partly hollowed out of the rock.

The interior is black and dismal; it looks like a dungeon in which religion is condemned to hard labor for life. Every stone in the pavement is a tomb-stone; and the dark images, carved in wood, and blackened by age, which are fixed against the walls, seem as if they had climbed up out of the high dark pews, and would go down again to the under world. Number Three turned back again to the sunshine, and, rejoining the two others, they ascended to the entrance of the great building—half abbey, half castle—the successive abode of monks, and soldiers, and prisoners.

We were on the eastward, or land side of the island, which is defended by a vast wall known as "La Merveille." We had ascended about two thirds of the entire height, and were standing before an old donjon, flanked by two battlemented towers. A flight of dark and steep stone steps leads to a black door in the donjon, barred with iron. A bell-handle hangs outside, with the inscription "*Sonnez*" under it. We rang, and were admitted by a young Jesuit monk, one of twelve who have been placed in the abbey by the Bishop of Coutances. We ascend more steps, and find ourselves in what it would seem natural to call an entrance-hall, except that it is really a crypt, with massive pillars and many doors, leading to other chambers. The one thing the reader must bear in mind is that this abbey is hollowed out of the side of the rock, and that, as you ascend from one story to that above it, you still find subterranean passages and rooms. You mount many dark steps, and find yourself in a dungeon. You emerge for a moment on a narrow platform of rock, which the industry of the early monks converted into a garden, and then you ascend again toward the summit, but find yourself still in the dark rock chambers.

It would be impossible to give the history of this building within our present limits, and yet it can not be passed over altogether in silence. The story is, that more than 1100 years ago St. Aubert, bishop of Avranches, resolved to build an abbey on this island, which some say was then the abode of Druids, while others assert that it was a sacred burial-place. It was known as Mons Tumba; and no doubt the peculiar reverence which was felt for it made St. Aubert wish to devote it to some sacred use. He believed that the Archangel Michael commanded him to build a monastery on the island, and that the command was repeated to him in vision after vision. He could not rest until he set to work; therefore, in 709, he led a small colony of Benedictine monks thither. Miraculous lights and signs are said to have pointed out the spot where the abbey was to be built, and the form it was to assume; and a spring gushed up to supply the monks with water. Not long after, we are told that priests arrived from a far-distant island, bringing the sword and shield of the Archangel. He had just destroyed a horrible dragon, which until then had ravaged their country, and had left these trophies of his victories, when he returned to the skies, with orders that they were to be preserved in the new temple dedicated to him.

Those early monks must have had a hard time of it, hollowing their cells and their graves also out of the granite rock, and carrying basket-loads of earth to make a small garden on a rocky ledge. No part of their work, except that garden, can be now identified; but the abbey grew apace, and many men whose names are familiar to us gave it help and protection.

The pirate Rollo, become a Christian king, reinstated the monks of St. Michel when pirates had driven them from their abbey in 925.

Guillaume Longue-Espée and his successors took the monks under their protection, and enriched the abbey by their gifts.

It must have been well to do by the time that William the Conqueror set out for England in 1066, since it equipped six of the vessels of his fleet. William did not forget his Norman friends; and as that kind of charity which consists in the transfer of other people's goods is not peculiar to our own times, Mont St. Michel profited greatly by the spoils of the vanquished.

Crowds of pilgrims resorted to the island, and by their help the monks amassed so rich a collection of manuscripts that the abbey was known as "The City of Books." In order to guard their own possessions, as well as to give shelter to their dependents on the main land in the time of war, massive fortifications were raised, and by the end of the twelfth century the abbey had attained its greatest splendor. The trophies of St. Michel, the shield and the sword, had not been without influence over his followers, and in 1157 Abbot Robert was governor of the castle as well as head of the monastery.

In 1203, when Philip Augustus wished to punish King

John for the murder of his nephew, Arthur of Brittany, he laid siege to Mont St. Michel, which belonged to the kings of England, and burnt the abbey to the bare walls. But when he was master of Normandy he rebuilt the parts he had destroyed, and placed a fortress on that crouching rock, the sister island Tombeleine. It was in vain, two hundred years later, that the English besieged the castle; it proved to be impregnable, and they were compelled to retreat. In 1254 the holy king St. Louis made a pilgrimage to Mont St. Michel: a tradition still shows the room in which he sat with the monks at mealtimes.

It was Louis XI. who instituted the order of St. Michel, and presided at the first chapter in 1469. There were to be ultimately thirty-six knights of the order, but only fifteen were at first created. Louis XI. himself invested them with the insignia of their order, a golden collar inlaid with shells, to which was suspended a medal bearing an image of the Archangel. At a later period the number of knights was increased to a hundred, and at length the honor was bestowed so lavishly that the sign of it was known as the "Collar for every cur."

The monks of those days were traveling a downward road, and by the year 1615 the Benedictines of Mont St. Michel had become so immoral and dissolute that they could no longer be tolerated even in a Catholic country. They were replaced by monks of the order of St. Maur, and we have nothing further to tell, except that they were swept away at the Revolution, and the abbey was converted into a prison. It was used as a prison till within the last two or three years, but it has now been assigned to the Bishop of Coutances; he has installed a few monks, and it is once again an abbey.

"We are twelve," said our youthful guide, with a dreamy smile, "the number of the apostles."

The bishop has also sent some nuns, who have charge of an orphanage outside the walls, near the parish church of which we have already spoken.

Not long before the beginning of the French Revolution, Madame de Genlis took her young pupils, one of whom was afterward Louis Philippe, to visit Mont St. Michel. She gives an account of their arrival in the middle of the night, guided over the sands by men with flaming torches, who shouted to warn them of dangerous places on all sides, while above and beyond stood the fortress illuminated in honor of the princes. She speaks with pathetic feebleness of the "melancholy impression caused by all these new objects." We did not share her melancholy, or, if we felt it, it was not because the objects were new, but because they were old and effete, and the ardor even of our young guide could not make us believe that new life would ever kindle the worn-out frame before us, or that the monk's cell, and then the soldier's barrack, and last of all the prisoner's dungeon, could ever become more than a show-place to saunter through and wonder at, and fill with sad visions of the past, rather than with hopes for the present and the future. Still, by the help of our photographs, we will walk through this empty shell.

We are in the crypt, or entrance-hall, one end of which is lighted by a large window. Near it is a counter, and under glass cases there are photographs, rosaries, chaplets, breviaries, crosses, and such like, for sale. One of the twelve "brothers" stands behind the counter, with grave but kindly answers for all our questions. He suggests that we should see the place first, and choose our photographs when we return, as we must do, to this hall. We pass, therefore, to the Almoner's Hall, in which alms were formerly distributed to the poor, and then to the Buttery, where the large stores required for this purpose were kept. These three are the crypts, or lowest chambers in the building, and their massive pillars support the weight of the upper part, that is, of the external walls or projecting parts, for, as we have said, every successive story is honeycombed out of the rock. These three crypts are known as the "Montgomeries." They take their name from a Huguenot Montgomery who made an unsuccessful attempt to get possession of the fortress. He had gained an entrance, but was slain in the Refectory, while the followers who accompanied him were put to death in the outer hall. The Knights of the Order of St. Michel used the crypts as stables for their horses.

We ascend to the set of chambers above the crypts, and enter the Salle des Chevaliers, or Salle de Conferences, said to be the finest Gothic hall in existence. Three rows of plain solid stone pillars divide the hall into four naves; the capitals of the pillars are richly carved with vine, acanthus, oak-leaves, and a host of fantastic ornaments; and the vaulted roof has richly-carved terminal roses. This hall was formerly the chapter-house of the monks. Every year, on the 1st of June—the day on which the relics of St. Aubert were transferred from Avranches to the Mount—all the priors of the house who were scattered throughout France and England used to meet and hold a chapter.

In the fifteenth century the monks gave up their beautiful hall to the Knights of St. Michel, who from henceforth held their chapters in it. They also hung up banners and shields, emblazoned coats of arms above their stalls, and made the place bright with color and gold. Empty and clean, it stands now as a memorial of a long train of ecclesiastics and a great host of armed men who have talked, and listened, and plotted, and disputed within it.

We mount more dark steps to reach the old Benedictine refectory, in which St. Louis is said to have dined. It is a vast hall, divided into two naves by lofty pillars. Two enormous open fireplaces, great empty mouths, gape side by side at one end of it. The monks are busy clearing and repairing the walls, and mending the windows, and here, as elsewhere, trying to remove the traces of the long occupation of the abbey as a prison. The wooden partition which divided large chambers into dormitories, the flooring which converted them into two-storied rooms, are all going or gone. Gaping holes, heaps of broken wood, scaffolding, and tools, all tell of an attempted restoration. But the massive pile is unpromising material, and the felons have left a brand upon it not easy to be effaced. The great tread-wheel is one of the most noticeable things either without or within the abbey.

We are still climbing up the rocky mount, and are now near the summit, for we have reached the crypt which is beneath the church that stands upon the highest point on the island. Nineteen pillars support the weight of the apse. They are crowded together, without beauty of form or finish, and look like a herd of great patient beasts crouching under a heavy burden. A light as from a star gleams out among them, and our young priest falls on his knees before a black image of the Virgin, of miraculous origin, which is held in high repute. Wandering among these pillars in the "dim religious light," we drift into talk with him as to his vocation. The life he leads may seem, he tells us, quiet and dull, but he likes it—it is his vocation. Some men can do one thing and some another; he does not say this is the highest that he has chosen; other people may not think so; but it suits him—meets his needs. He is happy even now while he is young, and how much more contented will he be when he is old, and the temptations of youth and the love of the world are removed farther from him! "We must obey the will of God," he continues, "and if I see that it is the will of God that I should stand here and preach to this pillar"—and he laid his open hand against the cold stone—"I must do it. What is it to me that it does not hear, or answer, or show any sign of grace? It is only by a miracle that any human heart is touched. It does not concern me whether God chooses to perform a miracle, but it does concern me whether I do the work He has appointed for me." The words were spoken with great simplicity and earnestness, and Numbers One and Three, who had at first looked suspiciously at our guide, were touched by them, but still thought it a pity he should kneel down and worship a little dirty image.

From the crypt we pass to the old "Promenoir," or

cloisters of the Benedictine monks in the twelfth century. It is rock-bound on two sides, and the thick outer walls are pierced with windows at such a height that light enters, but no vision of the outer world. It is, in fact, a long dark vault, and a vaulted passage leads from it to the garden of the Benedictines—a ledge of rock, from which some of the stone had been hollowed out for building purposes, and to which all the soil had been carried up in baskets.

Beyond the cloisters are the *cachots*, the cells used for solitary confinement. They are known as "The Great Exile," "The Little Exile," and "The Devil's Call." They are all hewn out of the granite rock; the first two have no light, and air is admitted through a very small grating near the massive iron-ribbed door. You enter one of them, and a sea of blackness swallows you up. You can not see your hand before your face, or guess the walls that shut you in. The door is closed, and your heart sinks within you. You can not hear the voices outside, and a great horror of darkness and silence seizes you. In frantic haste you grope around and above, to make sure that no evil thing lurks to seize you. The place is empty, dark, hopeless; you shudder to think of the wretch shut up alone there with his crimes or his wrongs, and your brain is busy with the awful realities of the past, when the guide opens the door to ask you, with a smile, if it is enough. He tells us that when the building was used as a prison, refractory prisoners were sent to these *cachots*, or dungeons, for twenty-four, or, at the utmost, thirty-six hours. But the soldier monks were not so merciful!

Another of the *cachots* was known as "The Iron Cage," though it was in reality a wooden cage. Strong wooden bars separated one end of a long and narrow cell, lighted by a single window, from the other. It was in this cage that the journalist Dubourg, who had written against Louis XIV., was imprisoned. Here, too, he died, or, as some say, was devoured, still living, by the rats.

On the same level with the crypt, beneath the church and these cloisters and *cachots*, is the Benedictine burial-place of the eleventh century. It is also hollowed out of the rock, and we find that the nave of the present church is above us, while some one of these long, vaulted chambers was probably the first and early church. We pass through them, groping our way to the light which comes from a window in the outer wall. Near it a tall, handsome man, about fifty years of age, and with the look and bearing of a soldier, is busy with plans, and charts, and drawings. He is making investigations, our guide tells us, and we pass out to a rocky platform, or rather to a cell, three sides of which are formed by the rock; the fourth is open, and there is no necessity for guarding it even when the prisoners are at work, for the rock above and beneath is a sheer precipice, which would make escape that way impossible. By means of an enormous tread-wheel, which was formerly worked by the prisoners, provisions were thus raised to the summit. The iron tramway fixed against the perpendicular face of the rock, up which they were hoisted, the large gap in the rock itself, and the dim outline of the great wheel within, are seen, as I have already said, from the sands and from the main land. Near at hand the place looks like the skull, and the wheel like the teeth of a gigantic Death, ready to tear and devour its victims.

When we returned to the old burial vaults, the Frenchman, busy with his plans, to whom we had merely bowed in passing, stopped work to ask if we had noticed the dark recesses, and knew how far they extended? Now our eyes had been unable to pierce the gloom, and we had merely passed along what we took to be a dark and narrow passage. He lighted a taper, and carrying it to some little distance, showed us a large subterranean chamber leading from that in which we stood, and receiving no light from the outer world. The prisoners used it as a store-house for wood, of which there was still an enormous quantity in it. Our new guide climbed over the heaps of wood, which at the far end reached almost to the roof. Fantastic figures started out of the darkness as he passed, with the taper held high above his head; arms threatened and hands beckoned him, sullen forms crouched down, and shadows fled from him. He sprang from one projecting mass to another, rapid, agile, and sure-footed, until at length he had mounted almost to the roof, and the light of his taper was made dim by the distance and the height at which he stood. The large dimensions of the vault, its high arched roof, and the pillars which separated it from a long aisle running parallel to it, were suggested rather than revealed to us. He returned, and the blackness hurried after him and shut him out again.

He explained his reason for believing that there are corresponding vaults and recesses on the other side of the passage in which we stood, and pointed to the evident traces of a doorway which must have existed at some time in the solid masonry. But the whole of this part of the abbey is dead and buried, like the old Benedictine monks; their cloisters, their cemetery, their church, are the vaults above which the new structures have been raised. Part of the old cemetery has been used until recently as a store-house for potatoes. The potatoes were heaped up over the bones of the old monks, and on the dust into which they have mouldered.

"You have but to scrape the dust aside," said our informant, "and you find their bones—skulls, and arms, and legs without number." We were not inclined to scrape for their bones, and left the vast tombs in which the past lies dead and buried to turn toward the upper air.

Our way lay through the old cloisters again, and then up steps leading from it, with the rock for a wall on our right hand. At a certain point the rock ended, and masonry took its place. "That is the summit of Mont St. Michel," said our guide; "all that remains is above and on the rock!" We emerge into the daylight and the open air, and find that we have now reached the third or topmost story of the abbey. On this story there are the cloisters, dormitories, refectory, and library of the 13th century, and the church with its nave of the 11th and choir of the 15th century.

The exquisite cloisters, with their 220 pillars, are of the 13th century. What a contrast there is between their lightness, grace, and beauty, and the gloom of the old Benedictine cloisters we have just left! Windows in the western wall look over the sea to the setting sun, and the space inclosed by the cloister walls is open to the blue sky, which was an unknown region to the older monks in their dungeons. Here, for the first time, one can shake off the associations of the fortress or the prison. The lavish and exuberant decorations make one sympathize with the delight which the monks must have felt when they had worked their way up to the light. The exquisite tracery of the arches, the slender pillars, and the delicate and subtle carving of the capitals, filled our guide with something of the enjoyment and pride his predecessors must have felt in them. Still, as we sat in the sunshine trying to realize the meaning of the change, we found that there was no mistake about the renunciation of the earlier times. There was an actual giving up of every thing which makes life pleasant in order to attain a higher good—which they believed to be incompatible with the pleasures of this life. Whereas later, although the theory of incompatibility was not abandoned, the recluses did contrive to get all the good things of this life, and the enjoyment of them. But they did this violence to their consciences with such evil results to themselves and all around them, as the world has seen.

At this stage we drifted into talk about the Jesuit missionaries in China. Our guide was greatly interested in the subject, and so excited in discussing it that we never got him fairly back to any more immediate interests. We passed from the cloisters to the church, which stands, as we have said, on the summit of the island. The nave was commenced in the 11th century by the Abbot Hildebert, and is Norman; but the choir is much more recent, and very much of it belongs to the Renaissance.

All the rich decorations of the church were destroyed at the time of the Revolution in 1793, but there are still many curious bas-reliefs, which have, however, been removed from their original positions, and placed in the chapels of the choir. We were struck with one which represents five scenes from the life of Christ, the central and largest being the Crucifixion. The two thieves hang one on each side of Christ, and the soul, represented as a naked new-born babe, is escaping from the mouth of each. A merciful angel is waiting to receive the soul of the penitent thief, while that of the impenitent is keenly watched by a devil with horns and hoof, and a pitchfork held in an ominous and suggestive position.

I think that the relief of having escaped from the crypts and *cachots* beneath may help to account for our admiration of the lightness, and largeness, and beauty of the church. It is very bare, and has the look of having been swept and garnished.

Several years ago the restorations and reparation which had become necessary were confided to the prisoners, a fact which makes any detailed account of them superfluous. Over and above any thing that could by any possibility have been required, they erected some enormous pillars in the nave. Works of supererogation are always out of place.

We passed from the church to the rocky terrace known as "Beauregard," and now from the very summit of the island looked once more over the wide expanse of sea and land—looked a farewell that was not all regret. It is better to know that some things have been than that they are, and the great interest of Mont St. Michel must be that it is the monument of a past that is dead and gone; that the pious hermits, the wicked monks, the dissolute soldiers, and the prisoners, will return no more. We left the church and descended on the outside of the abbey buildings, passing the cistern under the northern transept, which contains twelve hundred tons of water. By many steps we reached the point from which we had started, and there in the entrance-hall, the first of the Montgomerys, we chose our photographs. The "brother" who sold them aided us with great intelligence, selecting the best he could find on the counters, and even then not contented until he had seen if he had no better copies in reserve. Had we not chosen too many? he asked. Did we want all those? Surely not the small size and the large ones also? Yes, we wanted them all, but should like the names written on them, lest we should forget. "I will fetch you a pen," said the *frère*, "and tell you the names. I would do it for you myself with pleasure, but I can not write." The announcement gave us as much surprise as if it had come from a curate in the Church of England, but it was stated so frankly and simply that we could no more have remarked upon it than if he had confessed to ignorance of the Zend Avesta. For all that, I am free to confess that I was dying to know *why* he couldn't write, especially as he was appointed salesman to the establishment; and if I ever go again, I mean to ask somebody else about it.

We said good-by to him and to our guide with regret, and once again turned our footsteps to the outer world, and toward the wall "La Merveille," by which we proposed to descend. There is now no garrison in the place; soldiers and criminals were removed together, and the marvel is, therefore, not that there are so few, but that there are any inhabitants at all, since there can be so very little occupation for them.

From the walls we looked down into gardens and houses beneath us, passed under mighty fig-trees, which in many places overshadowed the path, and longed for tempting grapes, which we stood and contemplated as they hung beneath us in delicious bunches. Now that special garden belonged to the male population of the island, namely, the brigand, who gladly recognized us, cut the grapes, and sent them to us by an old woman, who put a ladder against the wall, and handed them to us in a plate. As we were speaking to her, angry voices in an adjoining garden attracted her attention. She looked over the wall, burst into tears, and scrambled down the ladder, leaving her plate, with the franc in it, upon the wall. She turned back to explain: "*Mon Dieu! mon Dieu!* it is a daughter fighting with her own mother-in-law! I can not bear to see it." But we looked, and saw two women looking coarse and wicked; the younger one much more so than the elder. So far as we could make out, they were fighting for the possession of an old broom-handle. The daughter secured it, and, pushing her mother-in-law out of the house, proceeded to bolt and fasten doors and windows. To her disappointment, the old woman did not return and take up the struggle, but went away to her neighbors, and loudly bewailed her wrongs. In vain the daughter-in-law opened doors and windows, and defied her to return; the old woman would not even look at the house. At last the younger appeared at a door in the roof, which opened on the wall close to us, and passed out, singing in a harsh, triumphant manner. This scene dragged the little island back into real life, and showed it as it really is—a population of poor and ignorant people, with no other employment or trade than making shell baskets and pincushions, and a chance of now and then conducting a stranger round the walls. A quarrel like that which we had witnessed was an event of all-absorbing interest. When we left the walls, and walked up the narrow street beneath, we found every one discussing it.

The brigand awaited us at the inn. He had made up his mind that a friend of his with a boat should earn an honest penny by rowing us up the Coesnon to the main land; that another dear friend should assist; that he himself would accompany us; and that a still more intimate friend, the ostler, should also be of the party. We protested against the arrangement, but the brigand had secured his point by sending the carriage away over the sands, and we had to submit. He helped us into the boat with such vigor, and pinched our arms so dreadfully in the operation, that Number Three insisted on his being "bought off" before we started. So we gave him a *pour-boire*, and told him that he need not accompany us farther. He was quite contented with the arrangement, and stood on the bank shouting good wishes to us, and superfluous directions to the rowers. We left the island glorified in the rays of the setting sun—quite a typical island, outer walls to guard against all foes, outer waves washing the strong wall; within, the village rising house above house upon the rock; the aspiration of the village fulfilled, as it were, in the abbey, and the aspiration of the abbey in the church. But the completion of the church, the spire with the Archangel, is now wanting, and its place is occupied by a square tower with a platform, from whence the curious traveler may count church steeples, and towns, and villages, and curious islands in the sea. And the island is like the church tower; it is a place from which to look out upon the past—a past that is utterly at an end. That life in which soldiers and priests occupied the social heights, and all others merely crouched about their feet to minister to them, and drag out a wretched life sustained by their bounty, is gone forever. Nothing else has come to take the place of priest and soldier in Mont St. Michel. They are gone, but the ignorance and poverty which they called forth and fostered remain to testify against them.

Look at it from afar, however, and how the glow of sunset glorifies the place, and distance lends it new beauties! We were glad the brigand played us that trick, as we sat silent in the boat, and the golden island glowed like a vision, and then faded out into cold gray rock.

We had some difficulty in finding our coachman, who had given himself up to skittles and cider. He invited us to partake of the cider, and we turned away in such indignation that his companion said to him, "Are they princes?" The irony was not lost upon us, but we sternly walked on, and when the carriage at length overtook us the coachman was penitent, and tried to appease us by a present of walnuts which he stole from somebody else's tree.

Although the evening was far advanced, the threshers

whom we had passed were still at work. A large heap of grain lay near them, and the road was knee-deep in straw. Men, women, and children, their day's work over, sat laughing and talking. There was no longer a quadrille party as in the morning, but four women and three men stood in a row working like one machine with seven flails.

We went home very quietly, saddened by the dreary waste around us, and recalling little bits to tell Number Two. We did tell her, but she refused to chronicle the events of this day, and so it fell to the lot of Number Four to take up her pen. I now replace it in her more skillful fingers, and in my turn "subside."

CHAPTER IX.

AVRANCHES.—PONTORSON.—DOL.—ST. MALO.—DINAN.

How soon do we forget pain! How long do we remember pleasantness! This—is it strange? no; it is not strange at all, that the dreary day which resulted, not unfortunately, in the account of Mont St. Michel being written by Number Four, is now recalled by Number Two only as a quiet misty time, of which she is now oblivious of every thing except the exceeding kindliness that surrounded her, the sweet expression of the faces, the tender tone of the voices, English and French, for the *femme de chambre* in despair called in some English ladies to her sick charge. Who they were Number Two never asked nor knew, for they left next day, but she cherishes still the recollection of their gentle services, as well as those of the faithful little Frenchwoman, with hand so light, and heart so warm, and patience never failing, whom she will likely never again behold in this world. Whenever she thinks of Avranches she thinks of these, and still persists that the place was a pleasant place—not dull, only peaceful—though the most she saw of it was the rose-covered chintz of the bed-curtains and the odd parapet of the opposite house before mentioned. Ay, and though the one thing she came to see she did not see; and Mont St. Michel, with all its wonders and beauties, remains, and probably will ever remain, to her a Yarrow unvisited, a bliss unattained. But Avranches is a permanent remembrance, in all its sweet picturesqueness—a place where, it seems, the sun always shines; the great sweeps of forest-land keep unfaded their waves upon waves of vivid green; and the bay, with its gray, castellated rock of·St. Michel, and the long, flat island of Tombelcine, lies forever bathed in that glittering soft sea calm.

Nevertheless, as soon as traveling was possible, even Number Two was anxious to depart, for time was limited, and we were already nearly due at our tour's end. So One and Four took the law into their own hands; Four engaging to speak, and One to maintain a dignified dumbness, which implied any thing, and gave the weight of masculine authority to every thing, they set forth to find a vehicle which should take us easily and safely to Dol, the nearest point where we could reach the now desirable railway. Up and down the town they went, always seeming to come back to the same point—the market-place, where sat old women under old umbrellas, selling the oddest combination of fish and vegetables, with fruit rare and lovely to an English eye and taste—grapes, figs, melons, in unlimited quantity. At last they succeeded in finding another old woman, who had a carriage for hire, but who, on the strength of a husband in Paris, horses six miles out in the field, and a *vaurien* of a *cocher*, asked about three times as much as she ought to have done. A parley ensued. Voluminous French from Number Four, severe, solemn, Britannic silence on the part of Number One. "Monsieur could not think of paying such a sum—thought it exorbitant—was exceedingly displeased" (here Monsieur, responding to a

K

hint, looked as black as thunder, and as inflexible as three resolute Britons rolled into one). "There was, therefore, nothing to be done but to go elsewhere."

"Ah! *mon Dieu*," reconsidered the complaisant Frenchwoman, "that would be a great pity. She supposed Monsieur must have his way. Would he consider such and such a sum too much?" suddenly descending in the scale of charges so rapidly that Number Four immediately guessed how much these innocent-looking Normans were cheating us obnoxious English.

"No, Monsieur objected still; but perhaps a modified arrangement might be possible." And at last a bargain was completed, at which, obedient to another hint, Monsieur smiled, sweet as summer, and professed himself quite satisfied.

"Ah! Madame, *Messieurs les maris* have always their own way, *n'est-ce pas? Toujours, toujours!*" said the Frenchwoman, regarding quite pathetically "Madame" and her supposed husband. So Numbers One and Four, not disclaiming their unexpected honors, came back with flying colors, and sent Numbers Two and Three into fits of laughing over their graphic account of the scene.

But, punctual to the minute, the two horses, reported as hard to catch in their field as young buffaloes on a prairie, stood peaceably at the inn-door, guided by the *vaurien*, who seemed the mildest of blue-bloused Norman peasants. It was a sunshiny day, and even Number Two revived a little to the pleasures of traveling, the interest of perpetually new scenes, the amusement of watching curious forms of human nature, so diverse, and yet radically so much the same.

"The noblest study of mankind is man," and so we got into conversation with our *vaurien*, and gained a deal of information about every house we passed, the principal one being the most pretentious modern edifice, with corresponding grounds; the property, he told us, of a gentleman whom the neighborhood had dubbed "*Monsieur le Marquis de Chocolat.*" After that we passed into a region very pretty, but very desolate, with only an occasional house, or cluster of houses, breaking the monotony of the long line of road. Sometimes there seemed to be a little agricultural work going on. In one place we saw a group fit for a painter—two men and two women threshing wheat. Their figures, and the mutual rhythm of their flails, used alternately in perfect time, made a quartette that was quite a treat to both eye and ear. And here, too, we noticed, as Number Four has said, that women's rights in Normandy seemed to consist in working as hard as the men, or a trifle harder. At village cider-houses—alas! as numerous quite as our beer-houses—at cottage doors and street corners, it was always the men we saw idling about; the women were generally busy at work. Only once did we notice a group really doing nothing; but then they were actually old women, ugly as the witches in "Macbeth," and they sat in a gossiping row, perfectly happy apparently, round a huge manure-heap, which proves, what often occurred to us English, that there must be something very peculiar in the construction of French noses.

At Pontorson we ought, according to "Murray," to have seen something—a fine old church and curious mutilated carvings; but we saw nothing beyond the commonplace street, and the large, desolate inn-bedroom, where we took refuge from the warfare there was between two rival hotel-keepers for the possession of us unworthy during the hour and half that the horses had to rest. Except—yes, I remember—Numbers One and Three did nobly start to investigate the church-yard, but soon returned, having seen nothing more curious than a few grave-stones, on every one of which were carved queer ornaments, which they afterward learned were meant for large stone tears—and having found their sole object of interest in the singeing of a large black pig.

We had hoped to get fresh horses at Pontorson; but our *vaurien*, who seemed as weak and pliable as if he had been the greatest saint alive, altogether failed in his negotiations, and we had to go forward, indulging our tired horses as best we could, and trusting to fate that we should reach Dol somehow, perhaps in time for the train to St. Malo, whither, with a wild longing to find strength in the fresh sea-breezes, Number Two entreated to go. Bright was the sun, delicious the air, lovely the country that stretched out before us, yet for the first hour our minds were too wholly intent on our horses to enjoy any thing much. Crossing the little river Coesnon, we became aware that "We Four in Normandy" was now a misnomer. We had passed into Brittany, that curious and beautiful country of which its natives are so proud, and the remembrance of which they retained immemorially by fixing upon ours the name of La Grande Bretagne.

We need not be ashamed of the title. Descending from the carriage on a hill-top, tempted at last by the most magnificent blackberries that ever grew, we suddenly looked behind us, and beheld a view impossible ever to forget. An amphitheatre, miles on miles in circumference, lay below us—not exactly a forest, but a sea of waving woodland. The intermediate pasture-fields are all planted with apple-trees, so that the country is one huge orchard. What it must be when the forest-trees first burst into leaf, and the apple-trees into blossom, may be imagined.

But we can not stop either to admire scenery or gather blackberries. Is it not one of the sad things of traveling that the traveler, more than most men, "never continueth in one stay"—that the pleasant places are as fugitive as the unpleasant ones—mere pictures in a panorama that is always moving on? Like a picture, therefore, now looks this beautiful Breton country, with the women in queer Breton head-dresses flitting through it—always the women; since, as before said, they seemed much busier than the men. In the few villages we passed, they sat knitting in groups, with their children round them; and deeper in the country we saw them collected about the apple-crushing machines, or following the huge fruit-laden wains, or picking up the rosy-cheeked refuse that still lay at the foot of the half-emptied trees. They were not handsome, these Breton women—less so decidedly than the Normans—and they all seemed prematurely aged, probably with outdoor labor; and yet it was better to see them, big, strong, bucolic-looking creatures, in their rough, picturesque costume—better by half than the fine, flaunting, dirty, sodden-faced, gin-palace haunting women who are the mothers of our city population.

But the afternoon advanced, our horses grew slower and slower, and our hearts were sinking within us, when we saw in the distance an unmistakable town, surmounted by a cathedral tower, and not far from it a great long hill, crouching like an enormous beast, something after the shape of the Wrekin in Shropshire, only it was not so green, but had houses and gardens sprinkled over its backs and sides. This was Mont Dol, one of the curiosities of the district, from its queer form and the way in which it seems to lift itself suddenly out of the plain, just as the rock of St. Michel rises out of the sea. Indeed, being of the same formation, granite, it is supposed that Mont Dol was also once a similar island, and that the bay extended thus far. Its present margin, not far off, is so shallow, that, though the tide flows up almost to the doorsills of the fishing-cottages which ring it round, no boat can approach them. This we heard, but saw nothing, not even the celebrated Rochers de Cancale close by, where feed the innumerable oysters upon which all Paris feeds in its turn. Our whole minds were set upon catching the train, and returning to the bosom of civilization.

Civilization did I say? Alas! certainly St. Malo was not the place to go to for it. Of all the abominable towns I ever saw, St. Malo is the worst—at least a century behind any provincial town in England in the comforts, and cleanlinesses, and decencies of life. Ghost of M. le Vicomte de Chateaubriand, so sweetly sentimental, so charming in your devotion to your faithful Madame Recamier, so egotistically exacting of the luxuries and refinements of life, do you ever come back and haunt that hotel which makes its fame upon the room where you were born? A room we did not visit, nor your tomb either, Monsieur le Vicomte, you being no hero to us; but the four-and-twenty hours we spent in your native town were enough to sicken us of it for life.

Enough. Let us turn from the dark to the bright side: there is a bright side to every thing. Undoubtedly St. Malo is a curious place; a town built entirely on a little island in a bay, and crossed to from the main land by a drawbridge; fortified to such an extent that one feels as if one had been besieged, or was going to be besieged immediately; and to see ordinary life carried on therein, or to walk idly on the deserted ramparts, and gaze round on the placid sea, emptied of invading ships, seems quite unnatural. One expects, simply as a matter of completeness, the bombarding squadron of Admiral Berkeley, or the army of the second Duke of Marlborough, or the countless privateers that in the last war used to drop in and-out of the harbor of St. Malo, to pounce upon any innocent English merchantman, like a spider upon a fly. People say that a great many large fortunes were made at this time by Malouins, who have never quite liked to mention how they made them.

But what of the Four? We slept, we rose, we wandered idly hither and thither round the ramparts, where the delicious sweet sea-air neutralized other airs not exactly from heaven; we watched the tide creep over the "*sillon*," the space of sand between island and main land. Numbers Three and Four valorously set forth along the chain of half-sunken rocks or islets which stretched out seaward, the most part of which is covered at high water, and came back wet, enthusiastic, rather regretting that they had nearly escaped being islanded at the end there until the next low tide. Numbers One and Two contented themselves with investigating the town, buying charming Algerine baskets of a young Malouin, who was exceedingly proud of his English, and penetrating, so far as it was possible, into the castle, built by that most independent person, Anne of Brittany, who put over one of its towers the quaint inscription, "*Qui qu'on grognê, ainsi sera : c'est mon plaisir.*" Doubtless she had her *plaisir*—this Breton lady. And to this day you can not look at the general character of Breton heads without feeling that the race are born to get their *plaisir*, viz., their own way, in most things—of which peculiarity we had full experience before nightfall; but of this anon.

There were two or three ways of getting to Dinan, our next resting-place, which we were hungering to reach— by carriage, by diligence, or by boat. The first was a roundabout way; of the second we had had enough; the third, hearing that the scenery down the Rance was not unlike that of the Clyde in Scotland, we thought we would try. So, after a morning in which we had exhausted, we believed, all the curiosities of St. Malo, and certainly our own capacities for enduring its unpleasantness, we thankfully bade it adieu, leaving nothing behind that we regretted except one face, set off by her peculiar head-dress — a grave, sweet, strong Breton face, which I am sure had "a story in it," though the woman was only a *femme de chambre* at an inn. Millais might have painted it, or Miss Thackeray invented out of it one of her charming studies of French women, like *Reine ;*

and even an ordinary observer could not help feeling that such women would make mothers of a race that fully justified the tolerably good esteem in which the Bretons hold themselves, and no doubt deserve to be held. They are, we were given to understand, both more moral and religious, as a province, than many other parts: they keep the Sabbath more strictly at St. Malo than in any town in France. It is only to be wished that they would add to their godliness a certain quality which has been described as being "next" to it among Christian virtues—cleanliness, so that strangers need not be driven to the resolution, in bidding adieu to this most picturesque and curious place, never to set foot in it again.

It did feel almost like Scotland, settling ourselves on board the steamer, whence, after just catching a glimpse of Dinard opposite, and of the wide sea-view behind, we saw following after us what on the Clyde we should have called "a scud"—a sudden drenching shower, sweeping up from the sea in trailing skirts of rain, obliterating every thing for the time being. It will pass, we said, for our tour had been wonderfully fortunate as to weather; but it did not pass—rather darkened down. When we ceased rocking on the mouth of the Rance, and began sailing down between its banks, admiring them as much as we could between the fissures of combined umbrellas, the scenery certainly became more Scotch than ever, especially the rain. Slowly the shores, which might have been pretty in sunshine, vanished in the mist, and we devoted our whole energies to keeping ourselves from being soaked through. Meanwhile we watched a party of Frenchmen, apparently young *propriétaires* going to *la chasse*, which in this part of the country consists, we are told, chiefly in a splendid "get up" for the occasion. Certainly their toilettes were astonishing, and their game-bags so highly ornamental as to make it rather a satisfactory circumstance that, as we heard afterward, they are not often filled. But we had not much time for criticism, since, as soon as ever the rain began to show a settled determination to fall—not furiously, but with a persistent soak, such as we had never yet seen in France, our sporting friends retired under shelter, whence they never emerged during the rest of the voyage.

For us, we braved it out. There are worse positions than that of four resolute people, well happed and cheerful-minded, each ready to endure inconvenience, and to save the others from it, sitting together on the deck of a steamer, and trying to make the best of things. In spite of the blinding rain, we saw enough of the Rance and its scenery to show us that heather and fern might grow luxuriantly, rocks be tumbled about in charming picturesqueness, and waves run merrily into pretty pebbly little bays here in France as well as in our familiar North. And though, of course, the Rance is not equal to our river of rivers—the Clyde—still it is a very beautiful stream, and, spite of the rain, we were almost sorry when we found our engines suddenly stopping, and our voyage at an end.

Then ensued a scene which certainly never would have happened even in the most barbaric regions of Scotland. It seems the Rance requires to have its channel periodically cleansed, in order to make it navigable to Dinan.

Accordingly, within about four miles of that town the stream is dammed up, and traffic ceases, the rest of the route being taken up by road. We had arrived the very day before the waters were to be let on again, and accordingly we were turned out, a troop of bewildered passengers, to find our way on as best we might, by means of a row of half a dozen carriages—if such tumble-down vehicles deserved the name—that we saw waiting on the bank.

Instantly we were surrounded by a troop of natives, as wild in looks and speech as if they were South Sea Islanders. They vociferated, they snatched at our baggage, they clutched us by the arm, to enforce their requests that we would enter their equipages; indeed, the drivers of two began a regular stand-up fight for the possession of our unfortunate selves. How it was settled I know not; I only know that somehow or other we took shelter from the beating rain in an old "shandrydan" of some kind, in which the two insane-looking Bretons who mounted in front promised to convey us to a hotel we indicated. Accordingly, packed as tightly as possible, we started, dashing at a reckless pace along the high, steep river-bank, over which—though happily we knew it not—only yesterday a carriage had been driven, and one of its occupants drowned.

Still we felt not quite comfortable, especially as at every wretched cabaret we passed—and we passed about one in each half mile—the whole procession of vehicles stopped, and all the owners turned out to refresh themselves with potations of cider, or cider-brandy, said to be the strongest, nastiest, and most injurious form of alcohol made in Europe. Meanwhile their horses—the wiser and nobler animals of the two—quietly cropped the grass at the very edge of the dangerous path, and the passengers, shut in and helpless, waited patiently or impatiently, according to their temperaments, till the refreshment was over.

These pauses, lasting from ten to fifteen minutes each, somewhat lengthened the road to Dinan. But when at last we saw the town, our annoyances, dangers, and wrongs were forgotten. Imagine a bright, rapid river, about as wide as the Severn at Bristol, or the Tay at Dunkeld, running along between deep banks, till, on a sudden sweep, these rise into high rocks, upon which grows a white, cathedral-crowned town on one side, and a green suburb on the other. Connecting them, cut out sharply against the blue sky—it was blue now, for the rain had ceased—was the span of a huge viaduct, massive and solid, yet so exquisite in proportion that it looked as light and airy as if fairies had built it during the night, or as if it had not been built at all, but grown as naturally as the rocks and trees. In a breath we all exclaimed that Dinan was one of the very prettiest places we had ever seen, and every succeeding day (we staid four bright days, though on two of them it rained all day long) confirmed the impression.

"Pretty" is perhaps the best word. No Breton scenery that we fell in with is actually grand; its chief peculiarity is a general sense of green, sunshiny beauty—homelike, and yet novel. No wonder that, like Avranches, Dinan is much colonized by immigrant English, whom ill health or ill fortune has driven abroad for a time.

Not after the fashion of Boulogne and other places—it is too dull, too quiet a town for disreputable people. The little society here is apparently seldom afflicted with a greater sin than poverty; and in this delicious climate, in the simplicity of life enforced by a community so small that every body must know every body, and all his or her affairs, impecuniosity ceases to be much of an evil. This small colony of happy aliens, building their nests together on the highest point of the rock, and living in that friendly fraternity which is so difficult to get in England —gossiping a good deal, no doubt, and perhaps growing by force of circumstances a little narrow and isolated, but invariably kind to one another in trouble, and sympathetic in joy; also ready to welcome, heart-warm, any new-comer with their own tongue as they welcomed us —we will not write about them, but we remember them, and shall always think with pleasure of the little English circle at Dinan.

This day, alas! we were not under its protecting wing, or we should not have suffered as we did, in almost the only instance on our tour where the natives really set themselves to plunder the foreigner.

Arrived in the town, our vehicle stopped, not at the hotel we had indicated, but at another, which looked so dirty, so disreputable, that we declined to enter it, and insisted on being driven to the one we had named. Our driver refused, and declared that here, and here alone, could we go. Then ensued a fierce parley, in which all the Britannic spirit revolted against oppression, and all the Breton spirit determined, like Anne of Brittany, to get its *plaisir*. Number Four, as spokeswoman, in most decided and indignant French insisted on our being conveyed to the place we had bargained for. Number One expressed an opinion to the effect that all Frenchmen, nay, all foreigners, were—well, never mind! Number Three looked unutterable things; while Number Two sat, silent and worn out, until the enemy began to take down our luggage and turn us out of the carriage. Then her heroism broke down; she begged that she might be taken any where, on any terms, if only she might lay down her weary head in peace. So, out of sheer pity, a paction was made by the indignant three, and it was agreed that, for the consideration of five francs, we should be conveyed to the right hotel. Accordingly, the luggage was replaced, we solemnly remounted, and were driven—just round the corner!

Great was the wrath of the three, and hard to bear the grin of the delighted *cocher*, as he held out his hand for his fare. But it had been a bargain, and must, of course, be held to—John Bull never breaks his word; only when, with a satirical smile, which ran through the circle of admiring compatriots gathered to witness the altercation between the native and the foreigner, our driver suggested that Monsieur should add to his generosity by giving a *pour-boire*, Monsieur could stand it no longer. The five-franc piece came out of the indignant British pocket, and then the wrath followed in a burst.

"*C'est un vol!*" cried Number One, impetuously, and marched away. The rest followed, Number Four boiling with suppressed anger, Number Three scarcely less furious, and Number Two following after in a most humiliated and depressed condition, feeling that for her had been sacrificed not only francs, but patriotism, honor, and justice.

But we were safe in harbor. The landlady condoled with us, but said, of course, that no imposition was surprising, coming from *that* hotel. She gave us the best rooms in her own; within half an hour she made us so comfortable, hovering about us with her bright Breton face, pleasant and motherly, that we soon forgot our wrongs. Friends came about us, protecting us from the possibility of further cheating, and guaranteeing our respectability in the eyes of the hotel. We had an excellent *table d'hôte*, and the *salon* all to ourselves, where, if any one had seen the merry Four over a regular English game at whist, they would hardly have recognized the four grumblers at St. Malo and its dirt, the four forlorn voyagers under dripping umbrellas, the four ill-used travelers, victims to Breton rogues.

Not that I mean to say all Bretons are rogues, but they certainly are a rougher race than, for instance, the Normans. In their *patois*, too, there is, even to a foreigner, as great a difference as between the speech of Cockneydom and Yorkshire, and in their manners a still greater variety. They pride themselves upon being not French at all, but Breton; and certainly they hardly seem of the same race as the polite Frenchman of the Boulevards, with his small figure, sharp, smiling face, and voluble, mincing, high-pitched voice. The Breton, big, bony, rough-tongued, is really more like a Briton by far. And yet there is a strong antipathy between the peoples, as our countrymen informed us. Even the £40,000 per annum which the English are said to spend at Dinan has not reconciled the natives to their presence in the town. There are still disputes without end—in fact, a sort of permanent guerrilla warfare between them and us, which only a few days before had come to a climax. A party of English cricketers, returning from a day's pleasure at St. Servan, had rashly called a Breton *cochon!* which the *cochon* returned by a cut of his whip. Thereupon ensued a general fight, the remembrance of which was likely to rankle in the Dinan mind for months.

But we were not foreign intruders, prone to look with too critical eyes on natural faults with which we had no sympathy, nor were we disposed to call even our enemy of the neighboring hotel a *cochon*. So we accepted our blessings, and laid us down under the roof of our kind-faced landlady, and within a stone's throw of still kindlier friends, with a deeper feeling of peace than we had known since we left England. We had also another source of thankfulness—at Dinan we re-found our clothes.

And here for a word of tender warning. Let no rash Continental tourists, who have suffered as we once did by the incumbrance of luggage, think to save themselves by leaving it behind them, and roaming about even for a few days with only a hand-bag and "what they stand in." No one knows his or her fare, especially in traveling. The misery of being exposed under pelting rain, knowing well that you have no other dress than the one you now sit and soak in; the dread of falling ill, and being detained at a hotel, and wondering what in the wide world you shall do while the *blanchisseuse* detains your garments, and makes you exalt the common comforts of your life into absolute luxuries—all these sorrows I pass over, because no one would pity them, or sympathize with the agony of waiting for telegraphic messages, the reckoning of the speed of the *grande vitesse*, the doubts as to whether French officials, to whom the matter can be confided, were to be trusted at all; nor shall I describe the thrill of happiness with which at last we stood over our welcome portmanteau, safe and independent of the world. Never, as long as we are in it, will we be left to wander over it without, at least, those "two changes of raiment" which Biblical authority has immortalized.

But our wanderings were drawing to an end. Numbers One and Two were already due to friends far off, Numbers Three and Four to others still farther. This day, on which, in the deep felicity of clean attire, we walked through the Sunday streets of Dinan to its cathedral service, the last Catholic church we were likely to have a chance of attending, was to be the final wind-up of the adventures of Us Four in Normandy. We felt a little sad, for all our holidays are rare, our combined holidays still rarer; and people who thus travel together for a whole week without quarreling, and actually regret one another at the end, must be, every body must allow, very peculiar, not to say estimable individuals. So, at first, we did not look at Dinan quite as admiringly as we ought to have done, from the regret that we should not see it properly together, since Numbers Three and Four were to depart quite early on Monday morning.

Still, the town struck us, on nearer view, with full confirmation of our first vision of it. A more picturesque place can hardly be; some of its streets are delicious in their quaint antiquity; and the square, with its formal trees, and its statue—ugly enough—of that ugly, improvident, heroic, affectionate, noble Du Guesclin, the grand hero of Brittany—is unique of its kind. Then there is the castle, built by the Duchess Anne, and now used as a prison (which we afterward went over, but not us " Four"); the Jardin Anglais, greatly boasted of, and certainly very pretty; above all, the viaduct, which makes a feature from all points of view, every point seeming lovelier than the last.

Dinan is a clean town too; probably from being set on a hill, so that its open street-gutters are less harmful than beneficial. If a storm comes—and one came just as we were quitting the cathedral—in five minutes the whole street is in a flood. We found ourselves islanded on a doorstep, and having to leap over a roaring torrent nearly three feet wide, unless we could wait for its subsiding, which we were told would not be for a quarter of an hour more. But it acted as a first-rate health-officer —no such abominable odors as at Coutances, Granville, and St. Malo troubled our sensitive British noses at Dinan. Instead, though it was Sunday, there was the rich perfume of peaches and pears attracting the respectable mass-goers as they turned home, and furnishing a picture like one of George Lance's at every street-corner. The fruit was not quite ripe, certainly, and, though it may seem heterodox and unpoetical to say it, I doubt whether open-air grapes, melons, or peaches are really half so luscious as our hot-house fruit, but they were most beautiful to look at. Though it was Sunday, we bought and ate.

Another Sunday expedition we made—our last—which will long remain vivid in our memories. The rain clearing and the blue sky coming back again—ah! that bright blue sky of France, seldom absent for a day—we determined to go somewhere, and some of us said, " Let us go to La Garaye."

Mrs. Norton's poem has made well known that touching story of a devoted husband and his beautiful loving wife, whom a sudden accident changed into a crippled invalid for life; how they turned their house into a hospital, and both gave themselves to the end of their days to the duty of succoring the afflicted, with not only their personal fortune, but personal care.

"The Lady of La Garaye" might or might not have been the lovely character Mrs. Norton has painted her, but there is no doubt that she and her husband were most individual and remarkable people — true philanthropists in an age when philanthropy was not the fashion; that they quitted entirely the gay world in which they were born, and hid themselves in this far-away nook among their sick, whom they personally tended. For this end they both studied medicine and surgery; and the Comtesse is reported to have been a famous oculist. They died—happily, almost a quarter of a century before the brutalities of the Revolution destroyed the fruit of their labors, and made the Chateau of La Garaye the ruin it is now.

We entered it, crossing a muddy field and still muddier wood, to a farm-house which is made out of some of its outbuildings, and inhabited by a tenant of the present owner, who turns what we call in England " an honest penny" by showing it to strangers. It is that most touching form of ruin—no castle, not even a baronial mansion, only a house. The gates of the garden where the Lady of La Garaye may have cultivated her medicinal plants are broken and lichen-covered; the gnarled apple-trees still bear fruit in their old age, and that day were a picture of rosy plenty; but over every thing is thrown the shade of desolation. Round the shattered windows, from which many a sick face may have looked out, gazing its last on this beautiful world, and many another brightened into health as it caught its first hopeful peep at the half-forgotten world outside—round these blank, eyeless windows climb gigantic brambles, trailing along heavy with fruit, as large and sweet as mulberries. Once more we gathered and ate—almost with solemnity. It was a subject too tender for much speaking about—that of a life which, darkened forever, took comfort in giving light and blessing to other lives sadder than its own—a subject that Dickens might have written about—Dickens, whom, as I set down his name here, I start to remember has been these twenty-four hours—*only* twenty-four hours—one of us mortals no more, but a disembodied soul.

"Oh, the solemn and strange
Surprise of the change!"

Yet how soon shall we all become shadows—those who are written about, and those who write—shadows as evanescent as the gentle ghosts which seem to haunt this ruined house, this deserted, weed-covered garden, which scarcely more than a century ago was full of life—life with all its burdens and all its blessedness, its work and suffering, pleasure and pain, now swept away together into eternal rest!

We staid a good while at La Garaye, until driven out of its pleasant solitude by the apparition of the cicerone, a grim-looking *fermière*, with hand extended for the customary franc. Then we left it forever, as one has to leave, in traveling, many a pleasant place, which one knows one is most unlikely ever to behold again with mortal eyes.

La Garaye was the last combined sight-seeing of Us Four. To be sure, after dinner, some of us wandered out, impromptu, to look at the town in its night aspect—rather dim, for the oil lamps are few, and even these never lighted when it is—or ought to be—moonlight. So the great gabled houses cast shadows black as Acheron, and the Cathedral, the *Seminaire*, and the Castle looked grand and gloomy as heart could desire. Only when we suddenly reached the edge of the Jardin Anglais, and leaned over the parapet which looks sheer down to the river's level—and I believe the rocks between which it runs are at that point fully two hundred and fifty feet high—the moon came out with a burst, and made the whole landscape as bright as day. It was a perfect fairy-land. I can not paint it—I can only remember. None of Us Four are ever likely to forget it all our days.

Next morning, when the long-absent rain, which had so kindly kept away from us, except in very brief showers, during all our tour, set in in one solid, persistent downpour, we parted. The less said of partings the better. If our readers are as sorry to bid good-by to us as we were to bid good-by to one another, I may say, with Mr. Pecksniff (oh! the sharp, sudden pain that comes with the allusion, the choking of the throat at thought of him who will never make us laugh or weep any more!), that "we have not labored in vain."

THE END.

VALUABLE STANDARD WORKS

FOR PUBLIC AND PRIVATE LIBRARIES,

PUBLISHED BY HARPER & BROTHERS, NEW YORK.

☞ *For a full List of Books suitable for Libraries, see* HARPER & BROTHERS' TRADE-LIST *and* CATALOGUE, *which may be had gratuitously on application to the Publishers personally, or by letter enclosing Five Cents.*

☞ HARPER & BROTHERS *will send any of the following works by mail, postage prepaid, to any part of the United States, on receipt of the price.*

MOTLEY'S DUTCH REPUBLIC. The Rise of the Dutch Republic. By JOHN LOTHROP MOTLEY, LL.D., D.C.L. With a Portrait of William of Orange. 3 vols., 8vo, Cloth, $10 50.

MOTLEY'S UNITED NETHERLANDS. History of the United Netherlands: from the Death of William the Silent to the Twelve Years' Truce—1609. With a full View of the English-Dutch Struggle against Spain, and of the Origin and Destruction of the Spanish Armada. By JOHN LOTHROP MOTLEY, LL.D., D.C.L. Portraits. 4 vols., 8vo, Cloth, $14 00.

NAPOLEON'S LIFE OF CÆSAR. The History of Julius Cæsar. By His Imperial Majesty NAPOLEON III. Two Volumes ready. Library Edition, 8vo, Cloth, $3 50 per vol.
Maps to Vols. I. and II. sold separately. Price $1 50 each, NET.

HAYDN'S DICTIONARY OF DATES, relating to all Ages and Nations. For Universal Reference. Edited by BENJAMIN VINCENT, Assistant Secretary and Keeper of the Library of the Royal Institution of Great Britain; and Revised for the Use of American Readers. 8vo, Cloth, $5 00; Sheep, $6 00.

MACGREGOR'S ROB ROY ON THE JORDAN. The Rob Roy on the Jordan, Nile, Red Sea, and Gennesareth, &c. A Canoe Cruise in Palestine and Egypt, and the Waters of Damascus. By J. MACGREGOR, M.A. With Maps and Illustrations. Crown 8vo, Cloth, $2 50.

WALLACE'S MALAY ARCHIPELAGO. The Malay Archipelago: the Land of the Orang-Utan and the Bird of Paradise. A Narrative of Travel, 1854–1862. With Studies of Man and Nature. By ALFRED RUSSEL WALLACE. With Ten Maps and Fifty-one Elegant Illustrations. Crown 8vo, Cloth, $3 50.

WHYMPER'S ALASKA. Travel and Adventure in the Territory of Alaska, formerly Russian America—now Ceded to the United States—and in various other parts of the North Pacific. By FREDERICK WHYMPER. With Map and Illustrations. Crown 8vo, Cloth, $2 50.

ORTON'S ANDES AND THE AMAZON. The Andes and the Amazon; or, Across the Continent of South America. By JAMES ORTON, M.A., Professor of Natural History in Vassar College, Poughkeepsie, N. Y., and Corresponding Member of the Academy of Natural Sciences, Philadelphia. With a New Map of Equatorial America and numerous Illustrations. Crown 8vo, Cloth, $2 00.

LOSSING'S FIELD-BOOK OF THE REVOLUTION. Pictorial Field-Book of the Revolution; or, Illustrations, by Pen and Pencil, of the History, Biography, Scenery, Relics, and Traditions of the War for Independence. By BENSON J. LOSSING. 2 vols., 8vo, Cloth, $14 00; Sheep, $15 00; Half Calf, $18 00; Full Turkey Morocco, $22 00.

LOSSING'S FIELD-BOOK OF THE WAR OF 1812. Pictorial Field-Book of the War of 1812; or, Illustrations, by Pen and Pencil, of the History, Biography, Scenery, Relics, and Traditions of the Last War for American Independence. By BENSON J. LOSSING. With several hundred Engravings on Wood, by Lossing and Barritt, chiefly from Original Sketches by the Author. 1088 pages, 8vo, Cloth, $7 00; Sheep, $8 50; Half Calf, $10 00.

WINCHELL'S SKETCHES OF CREATION. Sketches of Creation: a Popular View of some of the Grand Conclusions of the Sciences in reference to the History of Matter and of Life. Together with a Statement of the Intimations of Science respecting the Primordial Condition and the Ultimate Destiny of the Earth and the Solar System. By ALEXANDER WINCHELL, LL.D., Professor of Geology, Zoology, and Botany in the University of Michigan, and Director of the State Geological Survey. With Illustrations. 12mo, Cloth, $2 00.

WHITE'S MASSACRE OF ST. BARTHOLOMEW. The Massacre of St. Bartholomew: Preceded by a History of the Religious Wars in the Reign of Charles IX. By HENRY WHITE, M.A. With Illustrations. 8vo, Cloth, $1 75.

ALFORD'S GREEK TESTAMENT. The Greek Testament: with a critically-revised Text; a Digest of Various Readings; Marginal References to Verbal and Idiomatic Usage; Prolegomena; and a Critical and Exegetical Commentary. For the Use of Theological Students and Ministers. By HENRY ALFORD, D.D., Dean of Canterbury. Vol. I., containing the Four Gospels. 944 pages, 8vo, Cloth, $6 00; Sheep, $6 50.

ABBOTT'S HISTORY OF THE FRENCH REVOLUTION. The French Revolution of 1789, as viewed in the Light of Republican Institutions. By JOHN S. C. ABBOTT. With 100 Engravings. 8vo, Cloth, $5 00.

ABBOTT'S NAPOLEON BONAPARTE. The History of Napoleon Bonaparte. By JOHN S. C. ABBOTT. With Maps, Woodcuts, and Portraits on Steel. 2 vols., 8vo, Cloth, $10 00.

ABBOTT'S NAPOLEON AT ST. HELENA; or, Interesting Anecdotes and Remarkable Conversations of the Emperor during the Five and a Half Years of his Captivity. Collected from the Memorials of Las Casas, O'Meara, Montholon, Antommarchi, and others. By JOHN S. C. ABBOTT. With Illustrations. 8vo, Cloth, $5 00.

ADDISON'S COMPLETE WORKS. The Works of Joseph Addison, embracing the whole of the "Spectator." Complete in 3 vols., 8vo, Cloth, $6 00.

ALCOCK'S JAPAN. The Capital of the Tycoon: a Narrative of a Three Years' Residence in Japan. By Sir RUTHERFORD ALCOCK, K.C.B., Her Majesty's Envoy Extraordinary and Minister Plenipotentiary in Japan. With Maps and Engravings. 2 vols., 12mo, Cloth, $3 50.

ALISON'S HISTORY OF EUROPE. FIRST SERIES: From the Commencement of the French Revolution, in 1789, to the Restoration of the Bourbons, in 1815. [In addition to the Notes on Chapter LXXVI., which correct the errors of the original work concerning the United States, a copious Analytical Index has been appended to this American edition.] SECOND SERIES: From the Fall of Napoleon, in 1815, to the Accession of Louis Napoleon, in 1852. 8 vols., 8vo, Cloth, $16 00.

BANCROFT'S MISCELLANIES. Literary and Historical Miscellanies. By GEORGE BANCROFT. 8vo, Cloth, $3 00.

www.ingramcontent.com/pod-product-compliance
Lightning Source LLC
Chambersburg PA
CBHW031750230426
43669CB00007B/563